FROM CONFLICT
TO COOPERATION

HOW TO MEDIATE A DISPUTE
BY DR. BEVERLY POTTER

FROM CONFLICT
TO COOPERATION
HOW TO MEDIATE A DISPUTE

BY DR. BEVERLY POTTER

RONIN PUBLISHING, INC.

P O Box 1035
Berkeley, California 94701

From Conflict to Cooperation
ISBN 0-914171-79-8
Copyright © 1996 by Beverly A. Potter, Ph.D.

Published and Distributed by:
RONIN PUBLISHING, INC.
Post Office Box 1035
Berkeley, California 93701

Project Editor:	Sebastian Orfali
Cover Design:	Brian Groppe
Cartoons:	Phil Frank
	Creative Media Services

First printing 1996

9 8 7 6 5 4 3 2 1

Printed in the United States of America

US Library of Congress Cataloging in Publication Data
Beverly A. Potter
    From Conflict To Cooperation
    1. Careers.   2. Psychology
    I Title.

ACKNOWLEDGEMENTS

Thanks to Jeffrey and Cynthia Schwartz and Don Lieberman at Law Enforcement Training and Research Associates (LETRA) who taught me the "crisis intervention" approach to mediating conflicts. The experience and learning was invaluable. Thanks to Vicki Katz at DeAnza College Short Courses where I molded the techniques into a workplace application and to all of the managers and supervisors who participated in those classes. Thanks to Judy Moss at the Stanford University where I taught the staff how to mediate disputes. The Stanford staff who attended the mediation training were wonderfully supportive and helpful in further refining the application of the approach to daily work situations. Thanks to my partner and friend, Sebastian Orfali, for his help in finally getting this material into print. And a special thanks to you, my reader, for investing your time and energy into this book.

TABLE OF CONTENTS

CHAPTER 1

CONFLICT

MANAGEMENT

W henever people live, play, or work together there is potential for conflict. That's human nature. Conflicts within families, for example, are legendary—especially between spouses, between siblings and between parents and teenagers. Working out issues of authority and individuality within the close quarters of a home inevitably brings family members nose-to-nose.

Conflict also springs up between friends. The more energy and emotion people invest in a relationship, the greater is its potential for conflict. Friends sometimes disappoint one another in a variety of ways; they may also find themselves competing with one another. Both these situations can be the source of considerable strain.

The workplace is another fertile ground for conflict. People have different priorities and conflicting workstyles. And co-workers can find themselves pitted against one another for choice assignments or advancement. The more that people depend on one another to achieve their own objectives, the greater is the potential for conflict.

Even though work is supposed to be a very serious place where important functions are performed, people often become upset by seemingly trivial things. People get into conflicts when they believe that something or somebody is interfering with their achieving a desired goal. The frustrating interference can have a variety of sources. A person may have personal limitations, such as the inability to deligate, or the source may be interpersonal, such as when business partners have different priorities. Other times the source of conflict may be unexpected change, such as when a governing body makes a decision about the direction of a neighborhood, and the neighbors revolt. The way roles and relationships are structured in a business or family can be a barrier to individual goals. Even differing styles and values can give rise to conflict. In almost every case these causes are accompanied by poor communication. When this happens people tend to strike out in various ways, which usually provokes other people, and a conflict ensues.

A TYPICAL DAY AT WORK

Shirley:	This business magazine has an article about how to negotiate a two million dollar contract.
Husband:	Really? I'm impressed.
Shirley:	And this other magazine shows how to analyze the economic indicators and re-structure data feedback programs for maximum capital gains.
Husband:	Oh, how exciting! What did *you* do at the office today, Dear?
Shirley:	Oh, we spent the whole day fighting over who stole Myrtle's bagel from the office refrigerator.

Whatever the source of the conflict, the actual cause of the dispute is often perception—the difference in the way disputants see or think about the source of the conflict. In an ideal world, when a dispute arises the conflicting parties would meet, get a clear understanding of each other's view, negotiate a mutually agreeable compromise, and make a commitment to carry out the agreement conscientiously.

But this is not an ideal world. Typically, disputants avoid direct negotiation. Acting on a limited or even a completely incorrect understanding of each other's view, they may take their dispute underground which creates a situation in which personal victory and winning points becomes more important than reaching agreement. But disagreements swept under the rug don't stay hidden for long. They fester and grow into bigger misunderstandings and bigger problems.

CONFLICT CAN BE CONSTRUCTIVE

Conflict is not necessarily bad, and it doesn't necessarily indicate a failed interaction. In fact, conflict can be a catalyst for creating interactions that are more satisfying. It can benefit people by pushing them to make needed change.

CONFLICT AS A SIGN

By its very nature, conflict indicates a need for change. Its message is, "Things aren't working around here. We've got to do something different." When taken as a signal, conflict can be a constructive force that pushes disputants to voice their differences so that they can be addressed.

CONFLICT CAN BE AN OPPORTUNITY

TO CLARIFY EXPECTATIONS

It's amazing how often we are unclear about what others expect, which can result in working hard to satisfy a spouse or supervisor, only to fail because we've focused our efforts in the wrong place or in the wrong way. Unclear expectations can lead to misunderstandings and disappointments that fuel conflict. It is easier to get along with other people—even people you don't like or who are very different from you or whose priorities are divergent from yours—when you know what they expect of you and what you can expect of them.

TO BUILD COHESIVENESS

People who work together to implement a solution to a conflict tend to develop a sense of "we-ness." In ways not fully understood, resolving a conflict together produces a bond or sense of connection. Such cohesiveness promotes teamwork.

TO CREATE A PROBLEM-SOLVING ATMOSPHERE

People who work together successfully to resolve conflict gain confidence in their ability to solve other interpersonal problems. They tend to approach new difficulties with a problem-solving attitude.

WHEN CONFLICT IS POORLY MANAGED

Conflict itself is not a problem. It is a signal that an adjustment is needed. While solving the conflict presents the opportunity for people to clarify expectations, build cohesiveness, and create a problem-solving atmosphere, these benefits are not guaranteed. Achieving positive results does not come by chance—conflict must be well managed. Unfortunately, more often than not, it is poorly managed. A mishandled squabble can undermine team spirit and demotivate people.

REDUCES MORALE AND MOTIVATION

People tend to feel misunderstood and angry when conflict is poorly handled. They may feel that their concerns are not being addressed, or that people are taking their adversary's side. People who feel unappreciated or taken advantage of tend to be disgruntled. Unresolved conflict can lead to chronic agitation and annoyance, which poisons morale and diminishes motivation.

CONTRIBUTES TO JOB BURNOUT

Chronic conflict can generate a feeling that there is nothing one can do to resolve the problem. Feelings of powerlessness create the conditions for burnout, which is a kind of job depression characterized by a "why bother?" attitude and declining performance.

RESULTS IN LOWER PRODUCTIVITY

People caught up in a dispute often spend excessive amounts of time thinking about the conflict, which distracts them from their work. When disputants come into contact several times a day, such as in an office or at home, the conflict can intensify, with staff taking sides, for example. When people are upset and distracted, their performance usually suffers. A poorly handled conflict can easily get out of control, with virtually everyone in the environment getting involved to some degree.

PROVOKES MORE CONFLICT

A poorly handled confict usually results in more conflict. Emotional outbursts and cutting remarks have a way of lingering in people's minds. Dwelling on words said in anger, people are offended. Soon a new dispute has emerged which, if handled poorly, will probably generate more ill will.

HOW CONFLICT IS PUSHED UNDERGROUND

The most common reason for mismanaging conflict or pushing it underground is anger, which is usually a by-product of conflict. But expressions of anger, especially in the workplace, are largely taboo. Everybody is supposed to be nice and work in harmony. When you step into the office in the morning you are expected to become a machine. You are not supposed to be emotional or fret over petty issues like someone taking your bagel. You're not supposed to scream at people, laugh uncontrollably, or weep on the job. You are expected to be rational, logical, cool, and professional—which, of course, people are not.

This makes it hard to resolve disputes because it isn't nice to have them. Some especially "nice" people can drive you crazy because they are so "nice" that you can never say anything un-nice to them and you're bad if you do. This makes resolving conflict nearly impossible, because resolution requires that people talk about what's bothering them— much of which is not "nice." Some nice-guys are masterful in preserving their nice image while making anyone who tries to confront them look like a monster. The nice-guy invariably has many other people who agree that he is nice and you are hostile, aggressive, and a trouble-maker for saying anything not nice about him.

> ## Direct expression of anger and frustration is taboo in the workplace
>
> **It's unprofessional.**
> **It's seen as losing your cool or being petty.**
> **It frightens people.**

This taboo creates a widespread denial of anger and avoidance of conflict, and very few people have developed the skills required to negotiate a realistic settlement of differences. Instead, most people use manipulation, sabotage, insults, and sulking to get what they want.

When conflict threatens productivity, it's the manager's responsibility to intervene and mediate a resolution. But managers who must mediate conflicts among their staff may not be able to settle their own conflicts.

When conflict erupts among siblings, threatening to tear the family apart, it is the parent—generally the mother—who is expected to intervene. But many mothers don't know how to handle their own squabbles.

When conflict surfaces in the classroom, the teacher is expected to bring the warring students back to the lesson at hand. But many teachers have difficulty handling their own disputes. Even school counselors,

whom we would assume could mediate student disputes, find intervening in student conflict especially challenging. Surprising as it may seem,
training in mediation is rarely included in counselor training curricu-
lums.

CONFLICT MANAGEMENT IS A SKILL

Conflict management can be
learned, and that's what this book is
about. The conflict management process has two major steps. The first step
is to gather information about the nature and scope of the problem. The
second step is to mediate an agreed upon solution.

The nature of the problem refers to the major issues of the dispute.
The scope of the problem refers to the breadth of the problem. Who is
involved, for example?

SITUATION

**Jeff, a city recycling deputy, and Sheila, an administrative
assistant, had a big fight. Alice, the acting program director, didn't know what happened, but she knew she had to
restore peace. She talked to Sheila, then she called in Jeff.
Their conversation went like this.**

Alice:	I talked to Sheila about the big blow-up yesterday. She says you keep putting her down and dumping your grunt work onto her. Really, Jeff! Now, what's going on here?
Jeff:	Wait a minute! I'm not dumping my work on her. And I'm not putting her down, either! She said she'd prepare a flyer for me. Then when I took her up on it she had a fit.

Alice:	Listen Jeff, you know everyone does their own paperwork here. What makes you think you can dump yours on Sheila?
Jeff:	I *do* do my own paper work. The problem is Sheila. Oh, you're always on her side. You girls always stick together, don't you.
Alice:	There you go again, Jeff. Now, you're putting me down, too. Don't you ever call me "girl!" Do you hear me? You're out of line!
Jeff:	Oh, what's the use! You never listen to me anyway.

Rather than resolving the squabble, Alice's efforts undermined her relationship with Jeff and laid the foundation for further conflict between Jeff and Sheila.

SITUATION

Sally and her brother, Mickey, have been bickering all day. Their father has finally stepped in.

Father:	I can't take any more of this constant bickering. Mickey says you've been hogging the phone and he missed his call from the Little League coach. When I agreed to let you two get a phone *you* promised there wouldn't be any fighting over it. Now, Sally, why are you being so selfish about hogging the phone?
Sally:	I am *not* hogging the phone. The problem is Mickey. He just sits and waits for the coach to call—just like the wimp that he is. All he has to do is just pick up the phone and call. But, no, I'm supposed to not use the phone all day long while he waits for the coach to call. It is just a bunch of bull....

Father:	Watch your language, young lady! You know playing ball is important to your brother. You could be considerate for once.
Sally:	Gawd! I can't believe this. You're always taking that punk's side.
Father:	I talked to your brother and now I'm talking to you so that I can understand the problem here.
Sally:	Yeah, you really understand, brother! Like father, like son.
Father:	You're crusin' for a brusin'. I am your father and you will show me respect or you will go to your room.
Sally:	Gawd, you're incredible. Yes, sir! I'll go to my room, sir!

What do you predict will happen? Chances are that the conflict between Sally and Mickey will escalate. The father's attempts were of no assistance. In fact, he probably made things worse. What started off as a conflict between Sally and Mickey ended up in an argument between Sally and her father. The same thing happened when Alice stepped into Jeff and Shiela's dispute. How did this happen? Unwittingly, both Alice and the father violated several important principles of effective conflict management. For example, they each began the discussion by saying, "Shiela (Mickey) says you..." so that they came across as taking the adversary's side.

CONFLICT MANAGEMENT

I first encountered the approach to conflict management described in this book when I was a member of a consulting team that taught police officers how to handle civil disputes and family fights. For police officers this is the most dangerous type of call—one in which officers are frequently injured or killed. Intervening in a fight can be extremely hazardous. Statistics show that these sorts of fights can lead to homicides which the police often say they saw coming. Like the O. J.

Simpson case in which the famous football player was accused of killing his wife and her friend, the police had been to the house many times before the tragedy. The officers were there time and time again, and each time the situation escalated. All too often, officers go into these situations with little or no training. A team of highly skilled psychologists, specifically trained to handle family fights and other people-conflicts, would have a hard time with these situations.

Few police departments send an officer to a fight alone. Generally, two officers are sent to "415s" or "family fights" as they are often called. From the moment the officers arrive at the scene, they are in potential danger. The officers must get from their car to the building where there could be a set-up such as a sniper laying in wait.

Once at the door, the officers must get into the building, which is another challenge. Someone may be hiding behind the door and shoot

or stab an unsuspecting officer as he or she enters. It is not unusual for angry people to turn on the police. The next challenge is to get the fighting people under control. They may be running around, yelling and throwing things. One problem is that police officers will instinctively grab at the man, and often the woman, who only moments before was screaming for help, will defend her abuser. In hot situations, disputants can distract officers and get behind them where they can grab at an officer's gun. There have been incidents in which officers have been shot by the very person they were there to rescue.

And if all this were not difficult enough, police officers function under severe time constraints. Whereas a team of psychologists could easily take a couple of hours to handle such a crisis, police officers don't have that luxury. They get calls for help every few minutes. The crisis intervention method we taught allowed twenty minutes from arrival on the scene to leaving. This included approaching the scene, entering the building, getting the disputants under control, finding out how each person viewed the conflict, mediating an action plan, and leaving.

I shaped the techniques we taught the police into tools useful to people who must intervene in everyday conflicts found in the home, on the job, at the playground, in the gym, among friends and sweethearts—wherever people live, work, and play together. Many of the examples will revolve around the workplace, because for many years I taught this material to supervisors and team leaders. I've retained that focus because conflict in the workplace is particularly difficult. People have a lot invested in their jobs. Conflict on the job can be p a r t i c u l a r l y demotivating and set into motion the vicious cycle of burnout. On-the-job conflict drags productivity down and cuts into the

bottomline. Mistakes in handling other people on the job can have long-lasting consequences. Whether you are a disputant or a supervisor trying to intervene, it takes only a few outbursts to spoil your credibility. People tend to be more forgiving at home or in play arenas—they "cut you more slack," as the saying goes.

Disputes you will be mediating will not be of the same magnitude as those which police face. If there is a threat of violence, don't intervene. Call the police instead—it is their job to handle violence situations.

CHAPTER 2

PRINCIPLES OF GATHERING INFORMATION

$\mathcal{T}$he first step in mediation is to gather information on the nature (what) and scope (how extensive) of the problem. This is accomplished by interviewing *everyone involved* to find out how *each* disputant sees the problem. It is important to interview all parties to the conflict because when disputants feel they have had an opportunity to tell their side, they tend to be more cooperative and more willing to compromise. Failing to interview all parties to the dispute can undermine mediation because disputants who feel they haven't been able to tell their stories fully tend to feel more frustrated and are less likely to follow through on a resolution plan. This chapter covers basic principles for mediators when gathering information about the conflict. The next chapter will address specific techniques for getting information.

PRINCIPLE 1: BRING THE DISPUTANTS TOGETHER

The inclination of most people, even experts, is to separate the disputants and talk with each one individually. Interviewing disputants separately is appealing because most people fear losing control and getting caught in the middle of a verbal battle. But separate interviews with disputants can create several barriers to resolving the conflict.

TAKING SIDES

When you talk to disputants separately, it is easy to fall into the trap of conveying one disputant's complaint to the other, which can come across as though you are taking sides. This trap was illustrated when

Alice asked Jeff why he was "dumping" his grunt work on Sheila and again when the father asked Sally why she was "hogging" the phone. It is difficult to relay one disputant's position to another without sounding as if you are taking that person's side. Even when you choose your words very carefully so as not to sound accusatory or biased, the other person hears *you* telling the adversary's story. Separating disputants can undermine trust and credibility because each disputant is likely to suspect that you have sided with their adversary, making it more difficult for you to assume the role of impartial mediator.

EXAGGERATIONS AND FABRICATIONS

What do you suppose Jeff is thinking when Alice is talking to Shiela? Or what does Sally think when the father is discussing the argument with Mickey—in private? The worst, right?

These suspicions encourage disputants to exaggerate and fabricate to bolster their story. On the other hand, having one's adversary present during the conflict interview acts as a check, because disputants are less likely to exaggerate and deviate from the truth when the person they are talking about is listening. If the person does exaggerate or frabricate, the adversary will usually protest.

TIME-CONSUMING

Talking with disputants separately to discover the nature and scope of the conflict is time-consuming. Alice first talks with Shiela which takes at least ten to fifteen minutes, if not a lot longer. Then Alice must meet with Jeff, which takes more time. Then she might decide to talk with Shiela again about points that Jeff made. More time invested, but is the problem solved? No!

ASSUMING RESPONSIBILITY

The most serious repercussion of interviewing the disputants separately is a subtle one. When the father talked with the brother and then the sister about their dispute over using the phone, he implicitly assumed responsibility for the solution.

KING SOLOMON

King Solomon:	Why are you fighting?
First Woman:	This is my baby and she is trying to take it.
Second Woman:	She lies! It is my baby!
King Solomon:	You shall share the baby. I order that the baby be cut down the middle.
First Woman:	Oh no! Please no, she can have the baby. Please don't cut my baby!
King Solomon:	The baby is yours. Take it home. [Turning to the second woman] You lied and are sentenced to 30 days in prison. [Turning to the guard] Take her away!

When Alice and the father talked with the disputants separately they stepped into the role of King Solomon. When you become King Solomon, you assume the responsibility for determining where the real fault lies and for proclaiming a fair resolution. Let's say that you manage to see the situation clearly and come up with an equitable solution. But suppose your planned resolution doesn't work. Whose fault is it? It's your fault because, afterall, it was *your* plan that didn't work. When you assume responsibility for the conflict's resolution, the disputants' commitment to making your plan work is weakened.

In short, when you interview the disputant separately, the implication is that *you* are going to decide what action will be taken. Whereas when you interview the disputants together you set the stage for mediation and for the disputants to solve their own problem.

In light of all these disadvantages, why do people separate disputants? The answer is simple. If you bring angry people together, chances are they're going to start yelling at each other. And then who knows what might happen! The main reason people separate disputants is the fear of losing control. This bring us to the next principle.

PRINCIPLE 2: MAINTAIN CONTROL

There are a lot of ways to lose control. The disputants may get off the topic. Some people ramble on and on and never get to the point. In conflict management, you direct the interview to the issue at hand. Letting disputants bring up old issues from the past is another way to lose control. What happened in the past can't be changed because change occurs only in the present. Later we will cover techniques for keeping disputants focused on the here-and-now.

But, most importantly, angry people often forget their manners and act rudely. As disputants listen to each other tell their version of the story they tend to get angry again and interrupt with "I did not!" or "That's a lie!" Maintaining control when bringing disputants together is essential to prevent being caught in the middle of a verbal battle. Bickering and provocative behavior must be controlled.

Each disputant has a hidden agenda to persuade the mediator that he or she is the "good one"—the one who is cooperative—and that his or her adversary is the "bad one"—the trouble-maker and cause of the conflict. Toward this end, disputants will usually attempt to present themselves as reasonable while they try to make their adversary look bad. Often they will attempt to provoke their adversary into an outburst so that they can say, "See what I have to put up with!" Using loaded words, like—"This idiot here...," is a common way that disputants attempt to provoke one another. Other provocations include heckling sounds, sneers, and annoying expressions, exaggerations, and direct attacks on the disputant.

Rule of Thumb: Act firm and fast.

A lot of people figure that it's okay to allow a little of this because they don't want to seem too pushy. This "nice-guy" style is a big mistake. Be prepared to stop outbursts, remarks, exaggerated expressions and noises, loud sighing, drumming of fingers, and other provocations. Bickering and fighting are easier to stop in the beginning. If you allow a little, it will escalate. Don't wait until disputants get so worked up that someone yells or throws something. Act firm and fast! Allow no slack in a dispute interview. You've got to hold a tight, short, reign.

CONTROL TOOL: YOUR AUTHORITY

In conflict management your authority is a powerful control mechanism when used skillfully. If you are a parent, teacher, supervisor, coach, or police officer you have built-in authority. In other situations, your source of authority may be more subtle. You may be an expert in something relevant to the conflict. You may have seniority or previous experience. You may be older or a long-time associate. For some people, authority comes from their confidence. Interestingly, when you act with authority, people will see you as having authority.

Be Indirect

The word "control" has negative connotations. One image that may come to mind is one of someone being pushed around or constrained. "I told you to get over there and shut up!"

What happens when you try to control others directly? There seems to be a natural, perhaps automatic, tendency to resist direct attempts to control us. Consider the obedient family dog. If you grab its collar and pull, even the most compliant dog will usually put its heels in the dirt and resist.

Using a high degree of direct force in a dispute interview is not smart. If your efforts fail, you can have a problem because you've built up resistance, which can lead to a contest of wills. If you say, "Look, I'm your boss (mother, coach, teacher, principal) and I expect you to *do* what I say!" you've probably blown it.

It is much smarter to control disputants indirectly. Subtly project your authority without announcing it. Communicate your clout indirectly. Avoid direct exertion of authority, because angry people tend to resist it. When disputants resist your authority, there is a great danger that you'll be pulled into a conflict over control with one or both disputants. Avoid threating negative sanctions, such as withholding something desired by the disputants, or the possibility of reprimand or termination. Use the setting and context to indirectly communicate your authority and the sanctions you control. In other words, don't state your authority, let the situation do it.

Use The Setting

Meet the disputants in your office or workspace. Remember the grade-school bully who became a polite boy when sent to the principal's office? The setting of the principal's office signifies authority. The same is true of your office. You don't have to say, "I'm your boss." The disputants *know* that, and meeting in your office serves as a constant reminder without *your* having to mention it. You don't have to communicate your authority, the office does it for you. If you have a home office or study you might meet there because it sets a business-like tone. Parents often like to sit around the dining room table but that can pose problems which we'll go into later.

Make The Meeting Formal

Treat the meeting with the disputants as you would an important appointment. Hold the phones, for example. If the meeting is planned for a later time, set an appointment on your date calendar. Ask the disputants to do likewise.

Use Your Manner

Subtly but firmly communicate this message with your posture, expressions, and voice: "I expect you to cooperate by following my instructions."

CONTROL TOOL: FURNITURE ARRANGEMENT

Suppose you sit behind the desk with the disputants on the other side of it. After all, sitting across the the desk communicates, "I'm the boss." How much control does this arrangement yield?

When sitting behind your desk you project a high degree of authority, but with this furniture arrangement you have little control over the disputants' behavior because there's a barrier and the barrier is the desk between you and the disputants. Imagine what can happen. As soon as one disputant begins to describe his or her side of the story, that person is likely to turn toward the other, effectively cutting you out of

POOR FURNITURE ARRANGEMENT

view. Also, disputants seated side-by-side on the other side of your desk would be so close together than they could easily reach out to poke, pinch, or slap the other. Soon they are eyeball-to-eyeball and have forgotten about you—on the other side of the desk. As one disputant talks about his or her complaints the other disputant is likely to disagree. As they get angrier and angrier, they start wagging fingers in each other's faces. It is easy to see how an explosive situation can develop.

How can you, the mediator, stop the bickering from the other side of the desk? The answer is that you can't without your exerting a high degree of force. You can raise your voice and yell loudly, "If you don't shut up, I'm going to write the two of you up!" Should the disputants persist in their arguing, you'll have to get up from your chair behind the desk and move to the other side of the desk to stop them. By that time you've lost control. It is better to never lose control in the first place, because it is easier to keep control than it is to lose it and then get it back.

 Rule of Thumb: It is easier to keep control than it is to get it back.

Suppose you put the desk or a table between the two disputants so that it is a barrier between them. This is an improved arrangement over the first one because the barrier prevents them from grabbing at each other. However, this arrangement doesn't solve the problem of the disputants' eye contact with one another. When disputants look at one another while telling their complaints they're likely to get angrier. In a psychotherapeutic setting it might be appropriate for the disputants to "encounter" one another. On the other hand, the purpose of mediation is to work out an agreeable plan of action so that disputants can function in harmony. Don't confuse conflict management with psychotherapy. This is not an encounter session—it is a focused and highly controlled problem-solving meeting.

POOR FURNITURE ARRANGEMENT

When disputants tell their respective stories, it is vital that they *listen to one another.* However, eye contact between the disputants is not necessary for hearing each others' stories. In fact, it might be problematic because when disputants look at each other while talking about their irritations with one another, they are likely to get angrier. Avoid this problem by keeping the speaking disputant's eyes *on you,* the mediator.

Rule of Thumb: Keep disputants' eyes on you.

A more powerful approach is to abandon the desk or table as a barrier between the disputants and use your own body as a physical barrier to the disputants' eye contact and to their touching one another. The way to do this is by sitting between the disputants, as illustrated below. As you will see when we explore using your body as a control tool, this furniture arrangement allows you the greatest flexibility while indirectly controlling disputants with your body position and gestures.

BETTER FURNITURE ARRANGEMENT

Where To Seat Disputants

Do not allow seating to occur by chance. Arrange the chairs for maximum control and take command when seating disputants. Use a directive, "Sit over here, George," and a hand gestures to guide disputants to sit where you can effectively maintain control.

Overstuffed easy chairs are designed to relax the people who sit in them. Use this principle. Use any lounge or easy chairs available. Seat the most angry or potentially threatening disputant in the deepest, softest, most comfortable chair available. Simply sitting in the soft chair will relax the disputant to some degree. And it is difficult to get out of an easy chair quickly when sitting deep into it which makes it more difficult for the person to physically strike out or jump up in an emotional outburst.

 Rule of Thumb: Seat the biggest, most dangerous, or most upset disputant into the deepest, softest chair available.

As mediator, on the other hand, *you should avoid sitting in an easy chair* because it will limit your agility and ability to control the disputants quickly. For one thing, softer chairs are more difficult to get out of, which means it will be harder for you to stand up quickly if you need to control the disputants more forcefully. Instead, you should take the straightest, stiffest chair for yourself.

If all the available chairs are of the overstuffed-type, don't sit back into your chair. Instead, sit on the edge of the chair. Don't lean back or cross your legs. Always *sit perched on the edge of the chair,* because it will allow you maximum control. When seated on the edge of the chair, with a slight bending at the waist, you can quickly move your body between the disputants to cut off their view of one another, for example. If the disputants begin bickering, interrupting, or otherwise threatening to get out of control, you can quickly stand between them without moving your feet.

PUT THE ANGRIEST PERSON IN THE SOFTEST,
DEEPEST CHAIR

Experiment with the feel of sitting in various chairs. Sit back and down into an overstuffed easy chair and cross your legs. Now get up to a standing position as quickly as you can and notice how many movements it takes to do so. Next, sit perched on the edge of the easy chair, with both feet parallel on the floor about as wide apart as your shoulders. Again, get up as quickly as you can while noticing your movements. As you do this experiment, it will probably become obvious that sitting perched on the edge of your chair allows you greater control because you can move into a standing position more quickly.

CONTROL TOOL: YOUR BODY

When there are only two disputants, which is often the case, seat them facing you, with one on either side of your knees. Then pull your chair up so that you are almost in between the disputants. With this arrangement, when one disputant begins to heckle the other, "Yeah, ape breath, tell her what you did next!" you can exert considerable control indirectly by merely leaning forward, while turning your back slightly toward the heckling disputant. With this small body movement you *cut off the heckler's eye contact with the other disputant,* which has a dampening effect on the heckler. Simultaneously, you communicate to the offending disputant that you are "turning your back on" that sort of behavior, which is another example of asserting control indirectly. The mediator's body position in the illustration on page 30 demonstrates this. It is important that while the annoying disputant *can't see* the other disputant, he or she can *hear* the other's story.

Generally, disputants will not touch or physically threaten you—the mediator. There are, of course, significant exceptions, most notably when the mediator has an intense personal relationship with one or more of the disputants, such as with family members—especially when a sibling intervenes between two warring siblings. If there is any risk or threat of violence, don't attempt to mediate. Call security or the police instead.

When disputants tell their side of the story they will often look at and speak to the adversary, instead of you. This can be a problem because when disputants talk to one another about the dispute they tend to get angry and resume the argument which can be a prelude to losing control. On the other hand, when speaking to you—the mediator—they will tend to be calmer and more cooperative. Accomplish this by

THE MAN GETS ANGRIER LOOKING
AT HIS ADVERSARY WHILE TELLING HIS STORY

keeping the disputants speaking to you don't let them speak directly to each other. Even though the disputants are not directing their comments to one another, *they can hear each other's story* because they are sitting there. This may be the first time each has actually heard the other's view.

What To Do

Use hand gestures and the positon of your body to control the disputants. If the disputant you are interviewing begins looking at the adversary, immediately tap your chest lightly with your fingers and say, "Talk to me. Talk to me."

THE MEDIATOR LEANS IN BETWEEN DISPUTANTS TO CUT OFF THE MAN'S VIEW OF HIS ADVERSARY AND TAPS HER CHEST WITH HER FINGER, WHILE SAYING, "TALK TO ME."

Typically the disputant will refocus his or her attention back onto you. If this doesn't work, then lean forward to block the speaking disputant's eye contact with the adversary while tapping your chest and saying "Talk to me." This positioning forces the disputant who is telling the story to direct remarks to you. By looking at you instead of his or her adversary, the disputant telling the story will be less emotional. In a therapeutic situation the therapist might actively encourage direct confrontation and intense expression of emotion. But this is not a therapy session. Unless you are a trained therapist or counselor you should avoid such confrontation.

 Rule of Thumb: Keep disputants talking to you. Don't let them speak to each other directly.

When you are sitting between the disputants and they become difficult, threatening to get out of control, you can quickly *stand up to exert greater force.* When you stand up you are immediately between the disputants. You can effectively control most disputants holding your hands with the palms down out about 8 to 12 inches from either side of your body and saying, "Hold on" and repeating the ground rules.

DISPUTANTS ARE GETTING OUT OF CONTROL

If necessary, you can increase your level of force quickly by raising your hands, with palms down, to about the height of your waist and saying, "Hold on" a little more firmly, followed by repeating the ground rules.

MEDIATOR REGAINS CONTROL BY QUICKLY STANDING UP
BETWEEN DISPUTANTS WITH HER HANDS OUT
AND RESTATING THE GROUND RULES

This seating arrangement also allows the flexibility to lighten up your exertion of control a little when the situation warrants it. If the disputants are listening without bickering and interrupting, you can lean back somewhat in your chair and allow them to look at one another while speaking. Should they subsequently begin bickering you can quickly increase your level of control again by simply leaning forward in between the disputants to block their view of one another once again.

CONTROL TOOL: GROUND RULES

Ground rules are *explicit statements of what you expect from the disputants and what they can expect from you.* Ground rules make people feel secure because they know what to do and what to expect. When someone deviates from the rule, you keep control because you can point to the ground rule as a standard.

Don't be wishy-washy: "Ah, I don't like to interfere but I think we might all benefit by talking about this. Don't you agree?" This is not a time to worry about being nice or chatting to break the ice. Setting ground rules is an effective way to start.

The following ground rule is effective in most conflict interviews:

GROUND RULE

I'm going to begin by finding out what happened. I will talk to you one at a time. I want to know how each of you sees the situation. [looking at Joe] *I'm going to listen to Joe's side first, then* [looking at Susan] *I'll hear Susan's story.*

Susan and Joe know what to expect and what is expected of them. They know you want to find out how each of them sees what's going on. They know that they will tell their stories one at a time and that they each will have a chance to talk.

If you begin to lose control during the interview, stop the disputants from talking and restate the ground rules in a firm voice. "Susan, right now I'm listening to Joe's side. I will get to you next." Or "Joe, I heard your side. Now I want to hear Susan's story."

It is easier to establish control immediately than to regain it after an outburst or argument. Establishing control right away by projecting your authority and laying ground rules to prevent outbursts and bickering.

There is always the question of who to interview first. There are no firm answers. You might have the most upset disputant talk first. The aggressive disputant, on the other hand, is likely to keep butting in with,

"That's not what happened at all!" Or, "When am I going to get my turn?" Or, "You don't believe that, do you?" It may well be better to have the more aggressive disputant tell his or her story first than to have him or her trying to override you. The aggressive disputant may be easier to control after having told his or her story.

Sometimes disputants will be of different ranks or status. Here it is probably wise to interview the higher ranking disputant first. Who you interview first depends on your judgment of the subtleties of the situation. The important thing is that *you* take control and decide who will go first.

Sometimes it's a good idea to play down the word "problem." Who wants to admit to having a problem—especially in a work setting or in front of friends, for example. You can substitute "situation" for "problem."

CONTROL TOOL: USE OF FORCE

The governing principle in using force is to *go from soft to hard.* Begin with a low level of force. Start in a gentle but firm manner and escalate the degree of force in your voice, words, and gestures as needed to control disputants. Avoid coming on strong in the beginning. People are generally offended by strong displays of force, so if you start with too much you can alienate the disputants, which makes it harder to function as a mediator. Sometimes a strong display of force can lead disputants to increase their level of resistance. For example, if you start off by shouting orders to the disputants in a loud, gruff voice, they may bolster their resistance and demand an explanation for your ordering them around, which could provoke you to order them more loudly and gruffly. If you come on too hard, it's difficult to back down.

> **Rule of Thumb:** Start off at a low level of force and quickly escalate to match the disputants' level.

Generally, to gain and keep control you should strive to match your level of force with that of the disputants. Then, when possible, lower your degree of force, as the disputants follow your direction and control themselves.

How To Use Hand Gestures

Hand gestures are powerful tools for exerting force. We understand this intuitively and use them frequently in everyday interactions. Pointing at someone you are talking to, especially when you move the pointed finger up and down, exhibits force, and generally people are put off by this gesture. As the mediator, you should always resist the urge to employ this common gesture. It comes across as scolding or lecturing, which is the opposite of the impartial attitude you should exhibit. It is antagonistic, and people tend to clam up or become hostile. On the other hand, a palm-up hand gesture, especially when you move your hand in a gentle, "come-hither" motion encourages a disputant to talk.

A palm-down hand movement towards disputant who interrupts or makes annoying guffaws or snickers puts pressure on that person to stop. The palm-down gesture can communicate a low level of force when used without turning your head or interrupting the person you're interviewing to communicate, "Wait!" or "Be quiet!"

MEDIATOR USES BODY POSTURE AND HAND
GESTURE TO CONTROL ANGRY MAN

You can increase the level of force in the palm-down gesture by looking at the disruptive disputant while extending hand in a "Stop!" gesture with the palm down. This gesture is universally recognized, across cultures. Even animals seem to understand the meaning of the extended hand with the palm out. Be careful not to use the offensive pointed-finger gesture which isa put-off to almost everyone.

MEDIATOR INCREASES LEVEL OF FORCE
BY TURNING HIS BODY TOWARD MAN, USING A FIRM VOICE,
TELLING THE MAN TO "HOLD ON," AND RAISING HAND
INTO A "STOP!" GESTURE

The level of force can be further increased by repeating the ground rules to the disruptive disputant while using the palm-down gesture. For example, you can say, "I heard your side. Now I'm listening to Joan's story." Or, "I'm listening to Joan now, I'll get to you next." A high level of force is communicated by standing up between disputants, with both hands extended and palms facing out while repeating the ground rules in a firm voice, "Hold on! I'm going to listen to you one at a time. I've heard Joan's story. I want to hear Mark's side now" (see page 27).

How To Use Your Voice

Pitch and volume of your voice can be altered to exert more or less force. The lower the pitch and louder the volume, the more force. Remember, when you make a strong display of force it is difficult to back down. Instead, use the control level appropriate to the situation. Remember the rule of thumb of starting low-key and escalating the degree of force to match that of the disputants.

PRINCIPLE 3: ESTABLISH RAPPORT

When an angry person is misunderstood or cut off in telling the story, he or she will usually get even angrier. You can tell this is happening when a disputant repeats the same complaint a number of

times, each more adamantly. If the disputant thinks you are continuing to misunderstand his or her side of the story, he or she is likely to lose faith in the process, refuse to participate, and may become more difficult.

When people feel mistrustful, they tend to clam up. Conflict mediation is difficult when people are mistrusting and closed. It is difficult to uncover the nature and scope of the problem, and it is difficult to get suggestions or agreement on a plan of action.

You can avoid this problem by establishing rapport. *Rapport is a feeling or atmosphere of trust characterized by harmony and agreement.* When disputants feel a sense of rapport they will be more open and forthcoming and more likely to tell you about the conflict. They are also more likely to participate in the resolution process of finding a workable plan of action for resolving the dispute. However, don't confuse having rapport with being "friends," which is an approach that will get you into trouble. The very definition of "friends" suggests that the people involved are not neutral parties. As mediator, your role is not one of a friend but as a concerned and neutral go-between.

WHAT DISPUTANTS REALLY WANT

Recall a time when you were a disputant in a conflict. When you told people your story, what did you want most of all from that person? While you probably would have liked it if he or she agreed with your side of the story, chances are what you wanted most was for the person to understand your side. Your job as mediator in the information-gathering stage is not to decide whose story is right. *Your objective is to understand each disputant's story as he or she sees it.*

When we get to information-gathering techniques in the next chapter, we'll explore ways to establish rapport quickly while avoiding the pitfalls of chit-chat and sympathizing. For the time being, remember that your objective is to communicate to the disputants that you want to understand each person's story as he or she sees it.

PRINCIPLE 4: DON'T AGREE OR SYMPATHIZE

Avoid reassuring, sympathizing, consoling, or supporting either disputant. Disputants will ask for your sympathy, and you may in fact feel a great deal of sympathy for a disputant's concerns. But showing this sympathy will inevitably look like you are taking sides to the other disputant. When a disputant feels you've taken the adversary's side, he or she will be less open to you as a mediator and might actively resist you. When you agree with one disputant you implicitly disagree with the other—even though you didn't mean to do so. Not only will the other disputant tend to feel put off to some degree, but sympathizing and showing support to either disputant subtly sucks you—which destroys your impartiality.

Frequently disputants will try to get you to appear to agree with them. Sometimes it is a tactic to upset the other disputant, other times the disputant is trying to get you to take their side without you meaning to do so. Generally the way disputants do this is by asking you questions that elicit your support and agreement. Consider the following.

❧

EXAMPLE:

Mediator:	What's the problem as you see it?
Disputant:	Shirley lost the requisition and the order wasn't filled. The client was furious. Naturally, I had to chew her out. You'd do the same thing, wouldn't you?
Mediator:	Yeah, I probably would.
Adversary:	You're always on his side!

EXAMPLE:

Mediator:	What happened?
Disputant:	He doesn't take messages on my calls and it costs me sales. So I told him to stay away from my phone. What would you do?
Mediator:	I don't know. It would certainly be annoying.
Adversary:	Oh, that's great! Well, I find this discussion annoying. Can I go now?

EXAMPLE:

Mediator:	What happened?
Disputant:	Whenever I correct her she starts crying. It's just a manipulation, don't you agree?
Mediator:	Could be...lot of women do that.
Adversary:	It's nice that you *men* agree, but I'm not going to sit here and listen to you two sexists!

In each example the mediator got off track when answering the disputant's question. The answers sounded like the mediator was agreeing with the disputant, or at least was partial to his or her view.

During mediation disputants tend to be hypersensitive to any indication that the mediator is biased.

Rule of Thumb: Ignore disputants' questions.

When you respond to these kinds of questions, you step into the trap and lose impartiality. Mediation is not a social conversation, and you don't have to adhere to rules of polite society that say you should always answer a question. In mediation you must maintain control. When you answer these kinds of questions you lose control. Instead, ignore the disputant's question and continue with the information-gathering process.

EXAMPLE:

Mediator:	What's the problem as you see it?
Disputant:	Shirley lost the requisition, and the order wasn't filled. The client was furious. Naturally, I had to chew her out. You'd do the same thing, wouldn't you?
Mediator:	Chew her out?
Disputant:	Yeah, she screwed up big and I had to set her straight.

EXAMPLE:

Mediator:	What happened?
Disputant:	He doesn't take messages on my calls, and it costs me sales. So I told him to stay away from my phone. What would you do?
Mediator:	Do you mean that today he answered your phone even though you told him not to do so?

Disputant: Yeah, he answered the phone and then
                   didn't take a message *again!* I've had it
                   with him.

EXAMPLE:

Mediator: What happened?
Disputant: Whenever I correct her she starts
                   crying. It's just a manipulation, don't
                   you agree?
Mediator: What happened *today?*
Disputant: She was telling a client on the phone
                   about the Johnson case and she had it
                   all wrong. When I corrected her she
                   started her ridiculous crying again.

PRINCIPLE 5: DON'T TALK TOO MUCH

Your objective in the interviewing stage is to gather information on the nature and scope of the conflict. It's difficult to gather information if you are talking. Instead, you should be listening while the disputants are talking. As a rule of thumb, the disputants should do about 80% of the talking while you do about 20% of the talking.

 Rule of Thumb: Disputants should do about 80% of the talking and you about 20%.

If you catch yourself doing more than 20% of the talking, you are talking too much, probably because of using poor interviewing techniques. You may be giving the disputants advice, having a conversation, lecturing, or second-guessing. The way to stick to the 80/20 rule is to use efficient information-gathering techniques described in the next chapter.

PRINCIPLE 6: DON'T BE INTERVIEWED

During the information-gathering phase you will be asking the disputants questions, one at a time, with the objective of understanding the nature and scope of the problem. At this point of the conflict resolution process, you should avoid answering the disputants' questions. There are always exceptions to this, such as when a disputant doesn't understand what he or she is to do, for example. Generally, however, answering disputants' questions tend to get you side-tracked from your objective of gathering information. Worse, you can lose control.

EXAMPLE:

Mediator:	What happened?
Disputant:	Ruth doesn't take supervision well. I have to explain everything five times, and then she still doesn't do it. I'm at my wits' end. Why does she do that? I mean, why can't she simply follow instructions?
Mediator:	Maybe she doesn't understand—you know, she's confused.
Disputant:	I don't know. I think she's got a problem with authority. Ruth thinks I'm her father or something. You know what I mean. You've seen the way she talks back to me, haven't you?
Mediator:	I don't know that I'd call it "talking back."
Disputant:	Well, what *would* you call it?
Mediator:	Maybe Ruth is trying to clarify, maybe you're not clear.
Disputant:	Well, maybe she's stupid and can't follow a simple instruction!

Ruth:	Well, maybe someone ought to ask *me*. This bozo thinks he's some great supervisor, but he doesn't understand anything and *that's* the problem!

By answering the disputant's questions, the mediator lost control. Instead of gathering information on how the supervisor sees the conflict situation, the mediator got side-tracked into speculating about the reasons for Ruth's behavior. Yet, the mediator hasn't uncovered the specific conflict that occurred today. Worse, Ruth, the other disputant, is listening to the speculations about her as she waits to tell her side of the story. Ruth is obviously alienated when she breaks in to suggest that they ask her about her motives instead of speculate. It may be difficult for the mediator to recover from this detour and get back on track toward the objective of gathering information.

 Rule of Thumb: Don't answer the disputants' questions.

The best way to avoid losing control is to ignore disputants' questions altogether and continue to gather information on the nature and scope of the conflict. If the disputant asks questions which indicate that he or she doesn't understand the process and what you expect, stop your interview and repeat the ground rules.

PRINCIPLE 7: DON'T LEAD DISPUTANTS

A leading question is a question asked in such a way that it leads the disputant to an answer you have in mind. Answers to leading questions can give a picture of the conflict which is more reflective of your preconceptions than it is of how the disputants' actually see the problem. Another danger is that you might lead disputants into areas which you think are potential problems but which the disputants don't consider a problem, thereby adding fuel to the conflict.

EXAMPLE:

Mediator:	Joe, what's the problem as you see it?
Disputant:	Jill uses my phone instead of going over to her desk. If that isn't bad enough, she doodles on my papers while she's talking!
Mediator:	Does she read personal papers on your desk, too?
Disputant:	Sure! How can she help but read them when she doodling her idiot flowers and boxes all over them. It's obnoxious. She has no right reading my papers.

Initially Joe was annoyed by Jill's using his phone and doodling on his papers. With the leading question the mediator lead Joe to add reading his papers to the problem. The mediator expanded the problem and may have fueled the conflict.

 Important Point: Most of our questions are leading and we are not aware of it.

Disputants know what's bothering them. You don't have to second-guess. Instead, use the effective interviewing techniques described in the next chapter to get the disputants' perception of the problem. *Remember, your objective in the interview phase of mediation is to find out how each disputant sees the problem.*

PRINCIPLE 8: AVOID CLOSED QUESTIONS

A closed question is a question that can be answered with "yes" or "no." The disadvantage of closed questions is that when disputants can answer questions with one word, ("yes" or "no") the mediator tends to talk more than 20% while the disputant talks less than 80%.

Another problem is that closed questions are almost always leading. The structure of a closed question is such that it suggests a particular view and asks that you agree or disagree with it. For example, the question, "Did you feel angry?" puts forth the issue of anger and the disputant is asked to indicate whether or not he or she feels that way. It does not present the possibility of other feelings. It is leading because the mediator has brought up the issue of anger. Here's another example: "Don't you think that shutting down is the right course of action?" This again is leading. The mediator has lead the disputant to the question of shutting down, while other options are not mentioned.

Closed questions, used one after another, tend to become an interrogation. "Did you...?" "Did he say...?" "Aren't you...?" are examples of closed questions. If this were instruction on how to be a prosecuting attorney, the advice would be to use closed questions and avoid open questions in order to control the witness's answers and lead him or her to a particular admission. You've seen the courtroom dramas on TV or in the movies.

EXAMPLE:

Interrogator:	Did you go out on the night of the 15th?
Mrs. Jones:	Yes.
Interrogator:	Did you see the defendant that night?
Mrs. Jones:	Well, I did see him but....
Interrogator:	[Interrupting] "Just answer the question, "yes" or "no."
Mrs. Jones:	Well, ah—yes
Interrogator:	Isn't it true, Mrs. Jones, that you went out on the night of the 15th and you saw the defendant and....
Mrs. Jones:	Yes, but I....
Interrogator:	[Cutting her off] Good! My case rests, Your Honor!

PRINCIPLE 9: KEEP DISPUTANTS ON THE TOPIC

As mediator, it is your responsibility to control and direct the mediation process. Keeping disputants on the topic is essential, as it keeps the disputants and the process under control.

Disputants can stray from the topic in a variety of ways. They can ramble, for example, into unrelated problems, things that happened in the past, or descriptions of other people's views which leads to confusion and makes it difficult to determine how to proceed to mediating an action plan. When disputants ramble into unrelated issues, it is *your* responsibility as the mediator to cut them off and redirect their comments to the current conflict.

A common derailer is when disputants stray from telling their viewpoint of the conflict to describing how they think someone else sees the problem. Don't let disputants tell other people's views. If the other person's view of the problem is important, then include that person in the mediation and interview that person directly.

 Rule of Thumb: Permit disputants to tell only their own views of the situation.

When a disputant begins to tell someone else's view, interrupt and ask, "What is the problem as *you* see it?" Often one disputant will tell you how he or she thinks the other disputant sees the situation, instead of his or her own view of the problem. Generally when disputants do this, they look straight at their adversary while getting more and more agitated. "He thinks I'm just some fool who exists to do his bidding. And he thinks... ". You may have to remind the disputant to talk directly to you by leaning forward into his or her line of sight while tapping your chest with your hand and saying, "Talk to me. Talk to me, William. What is the problem as *you* see it?"

EXAMPLE:

Mediator:	What is the problem as you see it?
Sharon:	Lynn thinks we're incompatible office-mates.

Mediator:	Uh-huh.
Sharon:	She says that I talk too loud on the phone and keep the window open so she is freezing all the time.
Mediator:	Lynn, is that how you feel?
Lynn:	Yeah, I can't work with her in the room.

The mediator has let Sharon tell Lynn's story but hasn't found out how Sharon sees the problem. Later this can undermine an action plan because Sharon will probably feel she didn't get her side out and that the plan doesn't meet her needs.

BETTER EXAMPLE:

Mediator:	What is the problem as you see it?
Sharon:	Lynn thinks we're incompatible office mates.
Mediator:	Uh-huh. How do *you* see the situation?
Sharon:	She says that I....
Mediator:	[Cutting her off] Sharon, what is the situation as *you* see it?
Sharon:	Well, Lynn is hypercritical. She is constantly complaining about everything I do.

Other times disputants may tell how people not present in the mediation see the problem.

EXAMPLE:

Mediator:	What is the problem as you see it?
Bill:	Well, everyone says that Jack here is rude. He's always butting in on your conversation.
Mediator:	What else do they say?
Bill:	They think he's out of line—everyone does, you know.

The mediator is off track. Instead of finding out how Bill sees the problem, the mediator is allowing Bill to tell what everyone else thinks. Jack may feel talked about and attacked. It can generate conflict between Jack and other people not involved in the mediation. Meanwhile, Bill has not described his view of the conflict.

BETTER EXAMPLE:

Mediator:	What is the problem as you see it?
Bill:	Well, everyone says....
Mediator:	[Interrupting] How do *you* see the problem?
Bill:	Well, uh, Jeff is rude.
Mediator:	What does he do?
Bill:	He butts into my conversations and corrects me.

PRINCIPLE 10: MEDIATE ONE PROBLEM AT A TIME

Restrict your mediation efforts to one problem. If you can success-fully mediate an effective solution to that problem, disputants will be more motivated to tackle other problems. Even if there is a backlog of problems between disputants, it's best to *focus on one particular problem to begin with*. When you permit disputants to bring up several problems, they tend to become mixed, and the process becomes confusing. Fur-ther, you can end up in a situation where resistance over the issues of one problem interferes with successful mediation of other problems and the process comes to a standstill.

EXAMPLE:

Mediator:	What's the problem as you see it?
Disputant:	There are so many things I just don't know where to start.
Mediator:	Give it a try. List the four or five things that are bothering you most.

Disputant: Well, he's disrespectful to me. And he
                    takes credit for my work. His office is a
                    mess. And he's constantly late for our
                    review sessions. Uh...and his reports
                    are loaded with spelling errors. Is that
                    enough?

It almost sounds like the disputant is working at listing enough problems to convince the mediator that the other disputant is indeed a problematic person. Further, it is difficult to decide which is the most pressing problem, which makes it hard for the mediator to know where to start.

BETTER EXAMPLE:

Mediator: What's the problem as you see it?
Disputant: There are so many things I just don't
                    know where to start.
Mediator: What's the problem *today?*
Disputant: Well, he's disrespectful to me.
Mediator: Disrespectful? What does he *do?*

PRINCIPLE 11: FOCUS ON THE CURRENT PROBLEM

Disputants tend to bring up old issues to build their case, but doing so doesn't help to resolve the conflict. Disputants can do little about the past. Even when the irritating behavior has occurred every day for months or years, there is little to be gained by reviewing the past offenses. A lot can be lost, however, because going through a litany of annoyances is sure to stir up disturbing emotions that can hinder mediation. The fact is that you can't change the past. Change happens in the present only, which means that if you can help the disputants make a change in a current problem, however small, this can set the stage for future problem-solving.

EXAMPLE:

Mediator:	What's the problem as you see it?
Disputant:	Well, it all began when I first got the job here about eight years ago.
Mediator:	Yes, what happened?
Disputant:	Well, he never said 'Good morning' and it was pretty rude. So....

The mediator has gotten off-track onto past offenses. Exploring a person's rudeness eight years ago does little for solving conflict today. Don't fall into this trap. Concentrate on what happened today (or in the recent past). When the disputant gets off the topic into other problems or things that happened in the past, interrupt with, "What is the problem *today?*"

BETTER EXAMPLE:

Mediator:	What is the problem as you see it?
Disputant:	Well, it all began when I first got the job here about eight years ago.
Mediator:	What happened *today?*
Disputant:	I was minding my own business and he just attacked me.

It may be useful to explore the history of the problem in psychotherapy or when commiserating with a friend. But tracing the roots of the problem is time-consuming and tends to get bogged down. And dredging up the past can get disputants more upset and derail the mediation process.

PRINCIPLE 12: REMAIN IMPARTIAL

In order to mediate effectively, the disputants have to feel that you are impartial. When a disputant feels you are on the other's side, that disputant tends to see you as an agent of the adversary and feels backed into a corner. When this happens disputants get defensive, hostile, or guarded, which makes getting information and mediating an action plan harder.

DRemain impartial and don't jump to conclusions. This principle seems so obvious that it hardly requires stating. But it is extremely difficult to implement because we naturally fill in the spaces and translate ambiguities into something familiar.

Rule of Thumb: Don't jump to conclusions

Without realizing it, you may draw unwarranted conclusions and communicate your bias. Disputants may think you've taken sides.

EXAMPLE:

Mediator:	What is the problem as you see it?
Jill:	Bob calls me these cutesy names.
Mediator:	Sexism is annoying.

The mediator jumped to the conclusion that the cutesy names were related to Jill's being female and that Bob was being sexist in using them. When Bob hears the mediator's conclusion he is likely to think that the mediator has sided with Jill. After that he'll probably be less likely to cooperate fully in the mediation process. The mediator could have avoided this pitfall by getting specific information.

BETTER EXAMPLE:

Mediator:	What is the problem as you see it?
Jill:	Bob calls me these cutesy names.
Mediator:	What names are those?
Jill:	After I brought a bag of French roast coffee beans he started calling me "Bean Head." He does this in front of the staff and clients. It's a put-down and not very funny!

PRINCIPLE 13: GET SPECIFIC INFORMATION

Getting specific information helps you avoid jumping to conclusions. The rule of thumb for getting specific information is to *go to the "doing level."*

Imagine the following scene:

> **Her chin dropped, but she quickly hid behind a narrow-lidded glance. However, her biting her lip as she intently twisted her pencil gave her true feelings away.**

Stop reading for a moment and recall the scene. What happened? What did you see? Did you see guardedness, ambivalence, vulnerability, or nervousness? Read the scenario again while asking the question, "What did she *do?*"

What did you see the second time? Did you see a dropping chin, a narrow-lidded glance, lip-biting or pencil-twisting? If you're like most of us, you probably made two different kinds of observations: inferences and specific behaviors.

INFERENCES	BEHAVIORS
guarded	dropping chin
ambivalent	narrow-lidded glance
vulnerable	biting lip
nervous	twisting a pencil

The second list of observations are behaviors or what the person is doing—which I call "the doing level"—whereas the first observations are inferences about the person's emotional state drawn from observing several behaviors. Making inferences works well when writing poetry or when telling your friend about a memorable experience. By their very nature, words in the inference column trigger images in the mind of the listener. Take "nervous," for example. For a few seconds imagine a nervous person. Chances are various images of a nervous person come to mind and you could probably describe that person in considerable detail. The problem for conflict mediators is that people's images of a nervous person can vary dramatically. The result is that it is difficult to get people—especially people in conflict with one another—to agree on what actually occurred. Was the woman described above nervous, or was she ambivalent? We could argue the merits of each inference.

Hearing behavior descriptions or "doing" words also triggers images. The difference is that these images tend to be pretty similar. For example, most people imagine similar images when hearing the phrase, "He nodded and winked in approval." *When the disputants describe their conflict on the doing level, you and they get a clearer and more consistent picture of the problem.* Consider again the nervous woman described above. While people are likely to debate whether she was ambivalent or nervous, they will probably agree that she bit her lip.

GO TO THE DOING LEVEL

Bring to mind another nervous person and observe this person in your mind's eye. What is he or she *doing?* You probably observed several behaviors. For example, he may have been pacing the floor, giggling nervously, tapping his foot, shaking his leg, wringing his hands, twisting his sideburns, or breathing shallowly. It is easy to come up with a long list of nervous behaviors that one might imagine. In other words, inferences are drawn from several behaviors and become a short cut way of describing that group of behaviors. But this leaves lots of room for jumping to conclusions.

Consider the man in the illustration on the next page. What inferences do you draw when the man on the left clasps and twists his hands? Most people take these actions to indicate anxiety or nervousness. Now suppose the man clasps and twists his hands, then crosses his arms over his chest and pats his upper arms vigorously, while standing on one foot and then on the other foot. We usually read this body language as shivering from being cold. Now suppose the man clasps and twists his hands while hunched over, squinting his eyes, saying, "Hee!

WHAT IS THIS MAN DOING?

Hee! Hee!" under his breath. We generally read this as scheming. Clasping and twisting are "doings" in each situation. The combination in which the doings occur is what sends various signals about the meaning we infer to be behind the behaviors.

BEHAVIORS	INFERENCE
clasping and twisting hands	nervous
clasping and twisting hands, patting upper arms with opposite hands, while shifting weight from foot to foot	shivering
clasping and twisting hands while hunched over, squinting and saying. "Hee! Hee! Hee!"	scheming

What can happen is that we can see observe behavior—clasping and twisting hands—and infer that the person is nervous, then "see" nervousness in the person, when the person is actually cold, for example. Then you could describe the person in question to a friend. "Oh, he was really nervous!" The friend then infers that the person described as nervous engaged in other nervous behaviors that are part of his or her image of nervousness. When you think about the possibilities for jumping to conclusions and misunderstandings, the problems that these kinds of descriptions can cause between disputants becomes more obvious.

EXAMPLE:

Mediator:	What's the problem as you see it?
Disputant:	Bill jumped me when I came in this morning.

Before reading on, stop for a moment and imagine what Bill actually did. The possibilities are numerous. Bill may have confronted the disputant with a grievance. He may have made an insulting remark. He may have startled the disputant with a practical joke. If you settle for a description like "he jumped me" you, the mediator, may be thinking Bill did one thing, when the disputant means he did something else. The rule of thumb in getting specific information is to go to the doing level.

EXAMPLE:

Mediator:	What's the problem as you see it?
Disputant:	Bill jumped me when I came in this morning.
Mediator:	What did Bill *do?*
Disputant:	He was complaining at me before I could even get my coat off!

The mediator uncovered the offensive behavior by going to the doing level and asking, "What did he *do?*" The disputant answered with more specific information. As a result, the mediator was able to avoid jumping to conclusions about the problem with Bill. This is such an important point that it is useful to review a few more examples. Consider the following poor mediator:

EXAMPLE:

Disputant:	Alice is inconsiderate.
Poor mediator:	Is she always late?
Disputant:	No.

The mediator jumped to the conclusion that Alice is late. But inconsiderate can mean many things. Further, the poor response is a closed question that can be answered with "yes' or "no" so that the mediator gets very little additional information and will probably begin talking more than 20%.

BETTER EXAMPLE:

Disputant:	Alice is inconsiderate.
Mediator:	What did she *do?*
Disputant:	When she went to the cafeteria she didn't ask me if I want anything. I always ask her If I can get her anything. It's just common courtesy.

Instead of jumping to a conclusion, the better mediator asked what behaviors constitute being inconsiderate. The mediator used an open question starting with "what," which put pressure on the disputant to describe what Alice actually did.

EXAMPLE:

Disputant:	Larry is so insulting.
Mediator:	Does he put you down in front of others?

Disputant:	Well, that isn't what I was thinking of— 'course he certainly does that— and he tries to make me look like a fool all the time, too!

BETTER EXAMPLE:

Disputant:	Larry is so insulting
Mediator:	What did he *say?*
	What did he *do?*
	or
	What happened?
Disputant:	He constantly tells me what to do. I can't remember him ever asking me for my opinion.

Getting the disputants to describe the conflict in terms of specific behaviors has another important benefit which is setting the stage for mediating an agreeable action plan. "He's insulting" is difficult to mediate. For one thing, Larry may not mean to be insulting and may not realize that the disputant is insulted by being told what to do. Worse, Larry may be offended and hurt by being described as "insulting," which could make him resistant to mediation. If the other disputant says, "I want him to stop insulting me," it is not at all clear what the disputant wants Larry to *do* differently.

Rule of Thumb: Go to the doing level of the problem.

When the mediator helps the disputants to describe the problems specifically, on the doing level, it is easier to understand what is bothersome and what one can do differently. For example, when the disputant describes that problem as "He never asks me for my opinion," the stage is set for mediating an action plan that will succeed. A plan that specifies that Larry ask for the disputant's opinion in certain situations is more likely to succeed than a plan that specifies that Larry be less insulting.

Important Point: Getting specific information sets the stage for mediating an action plan.

Remember, disputants tend to present conflicts in ways that make them seem impossible to solve. They generalize, catastrophize, embroider, and exaggerate. To be effective you must cut through to the doing of the problem: What did the person *do* that was bothersome? By helping disputants state their complaints on the doing level you defuse emotion and begin problem-solving.

SOME BENEFITS OF GOING TO THE DOING LEVEL

> Defuses emotion
> Begins problem solving
> Makes the impossible possible
> Communicates impartiality
> Makes problem identification easier

Focusing on doing helps to transform the problem from impossible to manageable. The doing level allows more objectivity. It's on the doing level that successful negotiations take place, because people change by doing something differently.

PRINCIPLE 14: ACCEPT EACH DISPUTANT'S VIEW

Your goal in the information-gathering phase is to find out how each disputant sees the problem. It is very likely that the disputants will have differing perceptions of the problem. And these differing perceptions are, in fact, part of the problem.

Don't fall into the trap of trying to determine reality or judging who's right and who's wrong. Don't be King Solomon. Avoid judging or evaluating the disputants' perceptions, because it will destroy your impartiality. And in most situations there is no one "right" viewpoint. *Avoid questioning the validity of a disputant's story.* When you question the accuracy of a disputant's story you question his or her perception, which tends to put the disputant on the defensive.

Important Point: There is no right point of view.

When disputants feel judged they tend to edit out things that might make them look bad, and as a result you don't get their full story. Judging can set off emotional reactions which interfere with your efforts to mediate.

EXAMPLE:

Mary:	He bosses me around constantly.
Mediator:	You're just saying that because you resent authority.
Mary:	Oh come on! What's the use, you don't listen.

Remember, when you are judging you can not remain impartial. Judging requires taking a stand. Judging puts you, the mediator, into the role of King Solomon. Accepting the disputants' stories without challenge or trying to decide who is "right" is  difficult for many mediators. It sounds as if one is suppose to accept exaggerations, for example. Again, remember that your objective at this stage of mediation is to find out how each disputant sees the problem. If one disputant lies or makes unwarranted accusations, for example, the other disputant will object. You don't have to do so.

Many mediators feel uncomfortable accepting the disputants' stories because they feel that by doing so they are agreeing with the disputant. Accepting a person's perception does not mean that you, yourself agree with the perception. Remember the question you ask each disputant is, "What is the problem as *you see it?*"

Rule of Thumb: Don't question the validity of stories. Let the other disputant refute inaccuracies in the story.

A person's perception is his or her perception. A perception doesn't have to be "right" or accurate to influence a person's actions. And you can have a completely different view of the situation. In the mediation process your view should be withheld. The conflict is between the disputants, and it is their perceptions of that conflict that is relevant, not yours.

 Important Point: You can accept a disputant's view of a situation without agreeing with that perception.

Disputants' stories will be divergent. They have a conflict, and the conflict tends to arise out of the fact that they each see the situation differently. This is a given. Your objective at this stage of mediation is to find out how each person sees the problem.

Another problem with judging the disputants' stories is that it shifts the responsibility for solving the problem to you, the mediator. This is a set-up to fail because the disputants are less likely to be committed to the action plan and may even actively sabotage it. Instead, the disputants will sit back and expect you to take responsibility for resolving this and future conflicts.

Ask questions for clarification and to get specific information, but avoid questioning the story's validity. *It is futile and antiproductive to look for "reality."* People act on their perceptions of a situation, not on reality. Their perceptions are reality—to them!

We might assume that objective witnesses to a situation, such as a get-away-car leaving a crime scene, would see the same thing. However, it is very common for each witness to see something different. One witness may swear that the car was blue, while another will insist that it was green, for example.

Avoid becoming a detective. Simply ask each disputant for his or her story. Ask questions to clarify, get specific information and avoid jumping to conclusions.

An important side benefit of this approach to mediation is that while you mediate a particular conflict today, you simultaneously communicate that you expect disputants to take responsibility for their own problems with one another in the future.

> **Important Point: Mediation communicates that you expect the disputants to solve their own problems while teaching a process for doing so.**

During the interview phase of mediation each disputant tells his or her story, one at a time, while the other disputant listens. It is often the case that this is the first time they have heard the other person's story. When people get into a conflict they often stop talking to each other and jump to a lot of conclusions about the other person's motivation. Sometimes simply hearing the adversary's story is all that is needed to resolve the conflict. "Oh, you thought that is what I wanted? Good heavens, no! What I wanted was...." Mediation can't progress until disputants have heard each other's complaints. Information gathering is the starting point.

> **Important Point: Mediation may be the first itme disputants have heard each others' stories.**

Interviewing the disputants in each other's presence is efficient because at the same time that you are learning about the conflict and how each party views the problem, the disputants are also hearing each other's story. Not only does this save considerable time, but once all the stories are out on the table, you are ready to move right into mediation.

PRINCIPLE 15: DON'T MAKE SUGGESTIONS

Remember, your objective in the first phase of conflict resolution is to gather information on the nature and scope of the problem. This means that during the interview phase you are not solving the problem. Exploring solutions at this stage will only get you off-track.

In fact, as the mediator you should *never make suggestions*, even when it comes time for the disputants to find ways to resolve the conflict. Decisive, action-oriented people generally find it difficult not to make suggestions. It's against their problem-solving nature. Nonetheless, hold yourself back. Keep your eye on the objective, which is finding out how each disputant sees the problem.

Disputants will try to get you to make suggestions, but don't respond to their requests, because when you make a suggestion you've strayed from your objective. Instead, ignore the question and stick to your agenda of asking questions to get information.

EXAMPLE:

Mediator:	What happened?
Disputant:	She doesn't take supervision well. I have to explain everything five times, and then she still doesn't do it. I'm at my wits' end. What do you think I should do?
Mediator:	You could write your instructions down.
Disputant:	Yeah, but she wouldn't read them.
Mediator:	How about having her repeat the instructions back to you?
Disputant:	Naw, that doesn't work. I've tried that.
Mediator:	Perhaps you could ask her what the problem is?
Disputant:	Naw, doesn't do any good. She won't talk.

Mediator:	Have you taken a supervision class? There's a good one offered by HRD.
Disputant:	Yeah, I've taken classes over there, but it didn't help 'cause they're really mickey mouse and a waste of time.

By making suggestions, the mediator was side-tracked from gathering information and lost control. Without realizing it, by making suggestions the mediator assumed responsibility for finding a solution. The disputant dismissed the mediator's suggestions with the classic, "Yes, but...".

 Rule of Thumb: Ignore disputants' requests for suggestions

Ignore disputants' requests for suggestions. Remember the rule of thumb from the earlier discussion about maintaining control. Don't answer disputants' questions. This is not a social conversation in which etiquette requires that you answer questions. Instead, keep your attention on your objective of getting information. Ignore the request for a suggestion and continue with your questioning.

BETTER EXAMPLE:

Mediator:	What happened?
Disputant:	She doesn't take supervision well. I have to explain everything five times and then she still doesn't do it. I'm at my wits' end. What do you think I should do?
Mediator:	What happened *today?*
Disputant:	I showed her how to fill out the book and told her to bring it to me when she was finished. But she didn't do that. I just can't take it. She's always rebelling.
Mediator:	What did she *do?*

Disputant:	She went right ahead and shipped without letting me see the book first. And, of course she screwed it up! How would you handle such imcompetence?
Mediator:	What did she *do?*
Disputant:	She estimated the value on the retail instead of the wholesale, so the customer had to pay a lot more import tax. Now the customer is angry.

By ignoring the request for suggestions the mediator was able to stay focused on the objective of finding out the nature and scope of the problem. Furthermore, if the disputant tries to give a suggestion, cut him or her off while stating briefly that you will get suggestions later, and continue with your objective of getting information.

EXAMPLE:

| Disputant: | I've got an idea about how to handle this problem. We could.... |
| Mediator: | Good. Hold your suggestion, we'll get to that next. First, I want to understand how each of you sees the situation. Now, what happened *today?* |

Here, the mediator acknowledges the disputant for having a suggestion and reassures him or her that the suggestion will be heard, while keeping the process under control and on-track.

PRINCIPLE 16: ENCOURAGE DISPUTANTS TO EXPRESS THEIR FEELINGS

All conflicts have an emotional level. Often, however, disputants will try to downplay their feelings. Commonly, disputants will present a cool and rational statement of the disagreement that glosses over the hurt feelings below the surface. Other times, the emotion is hidden by not stating the problem in its entirety. When emotion is expressed it will often be annoyance or anger because hostility and other anger-related emotions are easier to express than hurt is. Most people find it easier to say, "You irritate me because you're so selfish" than to say than "I was hurt because I was not invited." Expressing emotions like hurt, disappointment, fear, guilt, shame, and lack of confidence make most people feel vulnerable and small.

> **Rule of Thumb: Inside an angry person is a hurt person.**

When emotions are denied, they tend to fester. People become increasingly sensitive to affronts by other people, even when the affronts were unintentional. Eventually, the situation produces an enormous gunnysack filled with hurts and annoyances ready to burst into new conflicts. Often, simply acknowledging the hurt feelings can avert this build-up of resentments. The mediator can help by recognizing the legitimacy of the feelings and encouraging the person to express his or her hurt. Acknowledging feelings builds rapport ("She really wants to understand where I'm coming from.") and increases the disputants' receptivity to mediation. A process that is not clearly understood, "owning one's feelings,"—which essentially is acknowledging the sad or hurt feeling—frees the disputant from the emotional hold of the feelings and allows him or her to negotiate with the other disputant.

Mediators should be careful, however, to not get carried away with exploring feelings. There is a certain sense of power and voyeuristic thrill possible with drawing out a person's hidden feelings. *The purpose of conflict resolution is to help the disputants make and carry out an action plan that cuts through the dispute.* Too much attention to feelings can side-track the process into an encounter or other kind of therapeutic process which the mediator is probably not qualified to conduct, and which may be at cross-purposes to the immediate objective of mediating an action plan.

CHAPTER 3

INFORMATION-
GATHERING TECHNIQUES

T he techniques that follow can be used to get good information quickly when you have little or no prior information about the disputants or the situation. You can use these techniques with two disputants, with several disputants, or when you yourself are a disputant. Maintaining control becomes even more critical when you have several disputants. We'll get to that later.

In the conflict management process your major information-gathering tool will be to ask questions. Like any tool, your technique can be more or less effective. When used with skill, the techniques that follow are "efficient" because they enable you to get a large amount of quality information in a short time.

TECHNIQUE: ACTIVE LISTENING

Active listening is the use of gestures, body language and sounds to actively communicate, "I am listening. I'm interested in what you are saying, and I'm working to understand your view." Active listening is not repeating or paraphrasing what the disputant said, which is an approach often used in a therapeutic or counseling context.

Active listening builds rapport. When you exhibit active listening you communicate that you are making a genuine effort to understand how the disputant sees the conflict. When disputants believe you are sincere in wanting to see their respective sides of the story, they will be more open and forthcoming.

You can communicate your desire to understand each person's viewpoint by exhibiting body language, such as nodding your head and by using the questioning techniques that follow to get and clarify information about the conflict situation. Don't try to be "a buddy" or become chatty, which will destroy impartiality and get you off course. Instead, simply focus on communicating the fact that you are listening.

NONVERBAL ACTIVE LISTENING

Giving the disputant your attention, *nodding, maintaining eye contact without staring, leaning toward the disputant, and palm-up gestures all show that you are listening,* and have a sincere interest in hearing the person's story.

Avoid frowning, shaking your head, shaking a finger, tapping your fingers, acting distracted, reading, or looking away. These nonverbal actions communicate irritation and disinterest and will sabotage rapport.

VERBAL ACTIVE LISTENING

Sounds like "uh-huh," "hmmm," "yeah," and phrases like, "I see," "go on," and "I want to understand" communicate that you are listening and want to understand the person's story.

Exhibiting active listening is somewhat of a habit. Everyone has a style of communicating, and some people show more active listening than others. If various people in your daily life often tell you something and then repeat it more insistently, you are probably not using active listening. As a result, other people think that you don't understand, you aren't listening or you don't care. If this happens to you, you will probably benefit from pushing yourself to exhibit more active listening. You can practice almost anywhere. When a co-worker, friend, or family member is telling you about something important to him or her, prompt yourself by thinking, "Okay, I've got to remember to nod (lean forward, say "hmmm," keep looking at her, etc.) to show that I am really listening and want to understand." Try this and you'll be amazed how positively people will respond to you.

TECHNIQUE: REPEAT

The technique is very simple. All you do is *repeat the ambiguous word or phrase* in what the disputant has said, *with a slight inflection* or rising intonation at the end of the phrase, which implies that the word or phrase is a question.

EXAMPLE:

Mediator:	What happened?
Disputant:	She was so rude, it was ridiculous!
Mediator:	Rude?
Disputant:	Yeah, she interrupts and completes my sentences.

The repeat technique helps you to clarify what the disputant has said by getting more specific information. You'll recall from the principles that getting specific information helps you to avoid the pitfall of jumping to conclusions. In most cases, the disputant will elaborate on the word or phrase that you repeated in more specific detail.

EXAMPLE:

Sandy:	This guy is weird.
Mediator:	Weird?
Sandy:	Yeah, he says funny things.
Mediator:	Funny things?
Sandy:	Yeah, he makes morbid jokes about everything.
Mediator:	Morbid jokes?
Sandy:	Well, you know, he's always predicting the worst-case scenario and then making fun of it.

Even though the mediator used only a few words, several penetrating questions were asked. "What about him is weird?" "What is funny about what he says?" and "How are his jokes morbid?" for example. Yet, each repeat was stated with an economy of words, thereby adhering to the 80/20 principle.

The repeat technique communicates "I'm listening," which builds rapport. The technique is very easy to use, and you can use it throughout the conflict-resolution process, thereby continually communicating your desire to understand, which builds rapport.

The repeat is effective with jargon, slang, and technical words as well.

EXAMPLE:

Wilma:	CAD simplifies my work.
Mediator:	CAD?
Wilma:	Uh, yeah, computer-aided design. It's a big break through.

Typically, the disputant will expound in greater depth on the word or phrase repeated. Often, disputants use more than one vague word or phrase in a statement. In this case, pick out the word you want clarified and repeat it. You can clarify the second ambiguous word or phrase with another technique later.

EXAMPLE:

Mediator:	What happened?
Disputant:	He mucked around in my trip and the lid blew off.
Mediator:	Mucked around?
Disputant:	You know, he started calling on my clients. Which is just not kosher. I guess he thinks I'm an idiot or something. But I'm not going to let him steal my clients.
Mediator:	You said "the lid blew off." What happened?
Disputant:	Well, I went straight to the District Vice President and gave him a choice. It's either him or me—and he better decide right now. He made the right choice. I'm still here!

You can interrupt with a repeat, and in most cases the disputant won't feel cut off.

EXAMPLE:

> Mediator: What happened?
>
> Disputant: I was just putting the finishing touches on the report when he came barrelling in here, shouting orders and insisting that I drop everything. So I....
>
> Mediator: Insisting that you drop everything?
>
> Disputant: Yes. He wanted me to put my project aside and help him make a 5 p.m. deadline.

The repeat technique is simple and straightforward. In fact, most of us already use it. Using the repeat helps build rapport, because the implicit message is, "Elaborate. I'm listening, and I want to understand what you mean by that."

TECHNIQUE: CHECK-OUT

The check-out technique is used to confirm your understanding of *what the disputant has said.* It helps you to avoid jumping to conclusions. The trick is to identify the conclusion you've drawn or assumption you've made and then to ask, "Do you mean...[+ your conclusion]?"

Perhaps you noticed that the question, "Do you mean...." is a closed question. A closed question is purposefully used because you want a "yes" or "no" answer. If you are correct in your conclusion, the disputant will say "yes" and possibly elaborate. That is, when your conclusion or assumption is correct, the check-out provides you with a confirmation. Then you can feel confident in your understanding, while at the same time you've communicated that you are making efforts to understand the person's story, which further builds rapport.

On the other hand, should your conclusion be wrong, the disputant will usually say "no" and then correct your misunderstanding with more specific information. Mediators often feel compelled to be "correct" in their understanding of what the disputant has said. Don't worry about being correct; instead, strive to use the check-out technique correctly.

Paradoxically, you get more information when you are wrong than when you are right! The reason is that when you use the check-out technique and are correct in your understanding, the disputant merely confirms it. Generally, you don't get more information. On the other hand, when the check-out and your understanding are incorrect, the disputant will almost invariably correct your misunderstanding with more specific information. In short, using the check-out when you've misunderstood helps you to build rapport because you've communicated, "I'm listening and want to make sure that I understand. Do you mean this?" and at the same time that you get more specific information.

So don't worry about being right, just strive to use the technique in the right way. Toward that aim it's very important that you phrase the check-out as a closed question, such as "Do you mean...?" in order to elicit a "yes" or "no" answer. Don't get lazy and say, "So what you mean is...?" which is not the same as "Do you mean...?" When you use the phrase "Do you mean...?" you are *asking*, which prompts the disputant to reply to your question. When you use the phrase, "What you mean is . . ." you are *telling* the disputant what he or she means, not asking. Telling a person how he or she feels can be off-putting to most people. Telling a person how he or she feels— when you are wrong in your understanding can be down right annoying. It takes an assertive person to speak out and correct your misinterpretation. The disputant may say nothing but think that you don't understand and don't care. This is counter-productive because you've drawn the wrong conclusions and don't realize it—and you've probably diminished rapport as well.

SPECIFIC CHECK-OUT

There are three types of check-outs: specific, general, and feeling. Use the specific check-out when the disputant has given general information or has been vague or ambiguous to check-out specific conclusions you might draw. Using the specific check out is a little tricky at first, but it gets easier once you get the hang of it. When the disputant makes generalized or ambiguous statements, *identify a specific example of what the disputant might mean*, then ask, "Do you mean [+ specific example]?"

EXAMPLE:

>
> Disputant: This place is a pressure cooker.
>   Possible meanings:
>   There are a lot of deadlines.
>   There's too much to do.
>   It's hot and humid.
> Mediator: Do you mean there are a lot of deadlines?
> Disputant: No, it's that there's too much to do and people are running around yelling at each other all day. I can't take it anymore.

EXAMPLE:

>
> Disputant: He's a nice guy.
>   Possible meanings:
>   He's friendly.
>   He's helpful.
>   He's generous.
>   He's easy-going.
>   He's a wimp.
> Mediator: Do you mean he's friendly.
> Disputant: No! He's a wimp. He let's everybody walk on him. He never says "No." But he's oh s-o-o-o nice!

GENERAL CHECK-OUT

It is easy to think that you understand what the disputant means when you are given a lot of details. This is a trap, because it is just as easy to misunderstand and jump to the wrong conclusion when you're given a lot of specifics as it is when the disputant is vague and ambiguous.

EXAMPLE:

> Disputant: Joanie leaves papers everywhere. There are overflowing ashtrays that make me sick and disgusting old coffee cups filled with mold sitting all over the place.

The disputant has given a lot of specific detail. But what is it about these things that actually bothers the disputant? It would be easy to jump to the conclusion that the problem is Joanie's messiness. To use the general check-out correctly, first *identify what the details* the disputant has listed *have in common.* In this example the common denominator might be messiness. The second step is to present your tentative conclusion to the disputant with a "Do you mean" question: "Do you mean [+ general conclusion]?

EXAMPLE:

> Mediator: Do you mean that Joanie's messiness is annoying?
>
> Disputant: She is a slob, but it's not that. It's just that she's just so inconsiderate. If she thought for just a minute she'd realize that I'm allergic to cigarette ashes and mold. But she never considers me. I'm just her assistant— her boy-friday.
>
> Mediator: Do you mean that the ashes and mold aggravate your allergies?
>
> Disputant: Yeah! I feel sick and foggy-minded all the time, and she doesn't care.

EXAMPLE:

> Disputant: I sew almost everything I wear and I make my own belts. I do pottery and make most of my dishware. I love planting things and often put bulbs in my crafted pots and give them as gifts.

> Mediator: Do you mean you like working with your
> hands?"
> Disputant: Yeah, I do... but *what I mean* is that I am
> creative while saving money!

The general check-out helps the mediator pull out the disputant's general concern from what at first can seem like a lot of unconnected complaints. When the disputant agrees with the check-out, the mediator can feel confident in his or her understanding of the problem. At the same time, the check-out helps the disputant to articulate his or her view of the problem more concisely.

FEELING CHECK-OUT

The *specific and general check-outs are used to verify* your understanding of the *content* of what the disputant has said and to verify your understanding of the *facts* of the dispute. The *feeling check-out,* on the other hand, *confirms your understanding of how the disputant feels* about what he or she is telling you.

The first step in using a feeling check-out is to *formulate a conclusion* or *theory about how the disputant feels,* then to tentatively ask, "Do you mean that you feel...[+ your conclusion]? Or, alternatively, tentatively say "I get the feeling that...[+ your conclusion]?

EXAMPLE:

> Disputant: Joanie leaves papers everywhere. There are
> overflowing ashtrays that make me sick and
> disgusting old coffee cups filled with mold
> sitting all over the place.
> Mediator: Do you mean that you feel repulsed by the
> way Joanie keeps the office?
> Disputant: No, not exactly. It is offensive, of course, but
> what really bothers me is the way she
> doesn't notice how it makes me physically
> ill.

Always be tentative when checking out feelings. Don't tell disputants how they feel, which can be experienced as pretentious or even invasive, and often puts people on the defensive. Avoid phrases like, "I hear you saying...." or "You feel..., don't you?" or "So how you feel is...." In each case you are telling the disputant how he or she feels. If you are wrong, the disputant must be assertive to correct you, but he or she may withdraw instead. It is better to say, "I get the feeling that...." or "I sense that...." or "Do you mean you feel...?"

 Rule of Thumb: Don't tell people how they feel or what they think; instead ask with "Do you mean you feel...?" or "Do you mean you think that...?"

A common error is to ask, "Do you feel...?" This question is leading, whereas "Do you *mean* you feel...?" is a feeling check. By asking, "*Do you mean* you feel...?" you emphasize that you are checking out your understanding of the feelings the person is expressing. Phrased as a check-out, the disputant is less likely to feel psychoanalyzed, and it becomes easier to correct you if you are wrong. On the other hand, "Do you feel...(angry, resentful, overloaded, etc.)?" is a leading question because it interjects your idea of what the person is feeling rather than communicating that you want to that you are confirming your perceptions of the feelings the disputant is projecting.

EXAMPLE:

Alison:	I was told to call Joe and that he would help me. But Joe says that he is taking comp time and that his boss made a mistake. I can't meet the deadline without Joe's help. It's important. And Joe's boss said he'd do it. But now that his boss is out on vacation, Joe gives me this story.
Mediator:	Do you mean you were depending upon Joe's help?

This is not a feeling check. "Depending" is an action, not a feeling. In the feeling check-out the mediator checks out his or her understanding of how the disputant feels.

BETTER EXAMPLE:

Mediator: Do you mean you feel let down by Joe?

Alison: Yes, I was depending upon him and now he won't help. I don't know what to do now.

EXAMPLE:

Shirley: We're just going around in circles and not getting anywhere. We've got to have a road map of where we're going in this report. We can't just start on page one and go to the end!

Mediator: Do you mean you feel we should make an outline?

Here is another example of confusing feelings and actions. Making an outline is not a feeling, it is an action. We often make the error of referring to thoughts and actions as feelings. That is okay in ordinary conversation, but precise use of words is important in a conflict interview.

BETTER EXAMPLE:

Mediator: Do you mean you feel uncomfortable with our unstructured approach to preparing the report?

Shirley: Yes, It is very confusing because I can't be sure of where we're going or what we're doing. I want to draw up an outline before we start writing in details.

EXAMPLE:

Robert: I try to do things the way Bill wants, but I just can't please him. He always finds something to complain about. And sometimes they're pretty silly things. So why should I continue to try? Just tell me that! No matter what a good job I do he'll find something wrong with it.

Mediator: Do you mean you feel you can't figure out what he expects from you?

Again, this is not a feeling check. Figuring out expectations is not a feeling but a thought process. Read Robert's complaint again. How do you suppose *he feels* about not being able to figure out Bill's expectations? One possibility is that he feels discouraged. Alternatively, Robert might feel angry. Either of these theories can be used in the feeling check.

BETTER EXAMPLE:

Mediator: Do you mean that you feel discouraged because you can't figure out what he expects from you?

Robert: Yeah! I mean, why try when everything I do is always wrong? It's very demotivating because I just can't win with him.

When To Use A Feeling Check-Out

It is important to remember that as a mediator you are not a therapist, and the purpose of mediation is not psychotherapy. In therapy, feelings are explored as part of the process of gaining insight into the dynamics of one's psychological workings. While this can be an important growth experience, self-exploration is not the goal of conflict mediation.

The dynamics of one's psyche is a personal matter. It can be distressing to have one's boss or teacher, for example, make psychological interpretations—especially in front of one's adversary. "What's *really* going on here is that you're still angry because Robertson got the assignment instead of you" is an example of psychologizing that comes across as judgmental and should be avoided. The objective of the feeling check out is to check out your *understanding* of how the disputant feels about the problem.

When The Disputant Gives Mixed Messages

Sometimes disputants will say one thing verbally and then contradict it nonverbally. *When body language contradicts the disputant's words,* you might use a feeling check out to comment on the contradiction.

EXAMPLE:

Disputant: [While frowning and clenching his jaw]
Well, I really respect her experience and knowledge. She's a great gal.

Mediator: I get the feeling that while you respect her capabilities, there are things she does that frustrate you?

Disputant: Well, yeah, I don't mean to complain, but she's so abrupt and pushy. It's hard to take.

Here the check-out focuses on the discrepancy between the words and the nonverbal message.

When The Disputant Is Reluctant To Describe The Problem

The feeling check-out can be particularly helpful *when the disputant seems to be having trouble talking about the problem.* Feelings of hurt or dissatisfaction, for example, can inhibit the disputant and be a barrier to mediation. When you help the disputant express these feelings, it may then be easier for the disputant to describe the situation that has triggered these feelings.

EXAMPLE:

Mediator: What's the problem as you see it?

Disputant: [While twisting paper and looking down]
             Oh, ah." Pause. "Well, ah....

Mediator: I get the feeling that it's hard for you to talk
             about this.

Disputant: Well, yes it is. He puts me down and makes
             fun of me.

Mediator: Do you mean you feel humiliated by his
             remarks.

Disputant: Yeah, I just want to crawl in a hole and hide
             when he talks like that about me.

When The Disputant Is Emotional

A feeling check-out can be helpful *with a disputant who is in a heightened emotional state.* A person who is crying and choked up has difficulty thinking, much less talking. Here, the check-out should focus on the emotion itself. You might say, "I sense it is very hard for you to talk about this." Or, "I get the feeling that it's hard for you to say how you really feel with Charlie listening."

Often simply acknowledging the feeling helps the disputant to talk about the situation. And, once again, you've built rapport by communicating an effort to understand.

When The Disputant Is Repetitive

Sometimes a disputant will tell the story over and over but not add anything new. It could be that the disputant has not expressed his or her central concern. People often resist stating their basic concerns, especially when they fear they will be judged as petty or immature. Instead, they will tend to accumulate a list of irritants and transgressions. Very commonly an irritant is used to express the emotion indirectly. If this is the case, the unexpressed concern will stand in the way of the conflict resolution.

While I've repeatedly emphasized that mediation is more effective when it occurs on the doing level, it is equally important that each disputant feels that the process addresses his or her central concern. When concerns are identified, then a plan for meeting the disputants' concerns becomes a practical matter of mediation.

The feeling check-out helps to get at such underlying concerns. First ask yourself, "What meaning do these irritants seems to have for the disputant? How does the disputant seem to *feel* about these events?" Then use a feeling check-out to tentatively pose your understanding of how the disputant feels.

To Neutralize Provocative Language

Be careful about how you describe the disputant's feelings, because the adversary is listening. It is important to choose your words carefully, because the feeling check-out that you pose to the disputant could come across as judgmental or antagonizing to the adversary.

EXAMPLE:

Roselyn:	Jack never helps clean the coffee area. He can't even rinse out his cup. He just leaves it moldy on the counter and uses someone else's. He expects me to clean up after him like I was his wife or something!
Mediator:	Do you mean that you feel taken advantage of by Jack's sexism?

Watch out! How will Jack respond to the mediator's comments? For one thing, "sexism" is an interpretation of the disputant's comments. Even if the disputant did use the word sexism, it would be unwise for the mediator to repeat it. Remember, avoid such loaded words, which is best accomplished by going to the doing level.

EXAMPLE:

> Mediator: Do you mean you feel imposed upon by
> Jack's leaving his cups for you to clean?

Consider the following complicated example:

EXAMPLE:

> Maud: She's constantly flirting with the men—
> playing helpless and batting those false eye
> lashes. I don't know how the guys can go
> for it. She won't give *me* the time of day.
> But then I'm not male and don't appreciate
> her assets, if you know what I mean.
>
> Mediator: Do you mean you feel that her flirting is
> disgusting?

This may appear to be a feeling check-out, but it isn't. The mediator has taken the disputant's words and turned them into an evaluative statement regarding her adversary's behavior. Chances are the flirtatious woman will be offended and get angry when she hears this check-out. It is imperative always to keep in mind that the *other person is listening.* Your job is to defuse emotion, not ignite it.

BETTER EXAMPLE:

> Mediator: Do you mean you feel disgusted by her
> flirting?

This is better but not optimal, because the woman in question is still likely to react to the words "disgusting" and "flirting." The mediator should translate these loaded words into neutral ones. For example, "offended" or "put off" are better than "disgusted," and "friendliness toward the men" is better than "flirting."

BETTER EXAMPLE:

> Mediator: Do you mean you feel put off by her friend-
> liness toward the men in the office?

This feeling check-out is much better because it acknowledged understandable feelings yet defused the loaded words. But has this feeling check-out really gotten to the disputant's core concern? Read her comments again while keeping in mind that people tend to exaggerate expressions of angry feelings while hiding hurt feelings.

BEST EXAMPLE:

> Mediator: Do you mean you feel left out because she is
> not as friendly towards you as she is toward
> the men?
>
> Maud: Well, the way that she acts like I'm invisible
> is really rude. I mean, I've been working
> here for four years, and I don't like being
> iced out like that!

TECHNIQUE: PROBE

A probe is an open-ended question beginning with "what," "when," "where," "who," "in what way," "under what condition," and "how." A probe is a wonderful technique because it cannot be answered with a simple "yes" or "no." For example, if the mediator asks, "Was Joe late again today?" the disputant can answer with one word, "Yes!" Such a closed question is problematic in a number of ways. Not only does it yield limited information, but it encourages the mediator to do more and more talking. Using an open-ended probe, such as "What happened today?" cannot be answer with a simple "Yes!" because it doesn't make sense. So the beauty of the probe is that it puts pressure on the disputant to talk, which keeps you with in the 80/20 rule.

CLOSED QUESTION	OPEN QUESTION
Is this situation interfering with your work?	What is interfering with your work?
Did he put you down?	What did he do?
Were you embarrassed by what she said?	How did you feel about what she said?
Do you think his actions hurt your credibility?	How did his actions impact you?
Wasn't she on duty at that time?	Who was on duty at that time?

Another problem with closed questions is that they tend to be leading. Without realizing it, the question, "Was Joe late again today?" was leading the disputant. In essence, the mediator was guessing that the problem today was Joe's lateness, then presenting it to the disputant in the form of a question. The problem today could be any number of things, such as not taking messages, for example. The probe, "What happened today?" doesn't presuppose lateness.

Rule of Thumb: Avoid leading questions.

A leading question is a question that leads the disputant to an answer or puts a particular frame of reference around the question. Such a frame can influence the disputant's answer. Learning how to ask open-ended questions that do not lead the disputant is one of the most difficult parts of the conflict-resolution process. However, once you "get it," the conflict interview becomes much easier because you are no longer under the (self-imposed) pressure to second-guess the problem. By using the probes that follow, you can pay more attention to what disputants are actually saying.

Let's look at several examples. How would an astute employee respond to the following questions posed by his or her supervisor?

EXAMPLE:

> Boss: Are you looking for more responsibility?
> Employee: Yes, of course.

It doesn't take much moxie on the part of the employee to conclude that the boss wants an affirmative answer. Considering the context of the situation, the employee would be foolish to answer in the negative— even if it were the truth. In short, the employee has told the boss what the employee thinks the boss wants to hear. That's why this sort of question is called "leading." Now consider a similar question restated as an open question.

EXAMPLE:

> Boss: How do you feel about more responsibility?
> Employee: Oh, more responsibility is very important to
>   me.

Again, it would be foolish of the employee to answer truthfully with something like, "Gee, responsibility really scares me. It pressures me tremendously so that I get very irritable." So while the question, "How do you feel about responsibility?" is an open-ended question, it is leading nonetheless because the boss put the issue of responsibility in the question which alerts the employee to the boss's concern. Because of the context of the question—namely, that it was asked by the employee's supervisor and bosses generally want employees to assume more responsibility—the question leads the employee to express a desire for more responsibility. In other words, simply using a probe will not guarantee that a particular question does not lead the disputant. This question is an example of what I call "putting the issue into the question." In this example, responsibility is the issue being discussed. It was the boss and not the employee who brought up the issue of responsibility by putting it into the question. Now, consider another question:

EXAMPLE:

> Boss: What are you looking for?
> Employee: Job security is a big concern of mine—I've got a mortgage to pay and kids to put through school. Then I like variety in my daily work.

This third question is an example of a skillfully used probe. The question is open-ended and can't be answered with a "yes" or "no." But more importantly, it doesn't alert the employee to the boss's concern. That is, unlike the previous question, which contained the issue of responsibility, there is no issue hidden in this question. The employee's answer is more reliable, because the boss didn't cue the employee to the issue of responsibility.

Part of the problem with leading questions is that most of us have a tendency to second-guess disputants and other people we're interviewing. This is very difficult to break out of but once you develop a habit of using truly open questions, conducting an interview—even when you have little or no information about the people or situation—becomes much easier. You don't have to guess what a person thinks or feels.

TWO POWERFUL QUESTIONS
"What happened?"
"What did he (she) do (say)?"

EXAMPLE:

> Disputant: Working with him is really a drag!
> Mediator: What happened?
> Disputant: He's always picking on me.

Mediator: What did he do?

Disputant: He's really insulting.

Mediator: What did he do?

Disputant: It's the things that he says. It's uncalled for.

Mediator: What did he say?

Disputant: He makes a lot of sexist comments.

Mediator: What did he say?

Disputant: He calls me "Baby." Can you imagine!

These two questions are powerful because you can get considerable information from a disputant even when you know nothing about that person or the situation. Additionally, you preserve your impartiality, because the questions are empty of issues—they are completely open. You don't lead disputants into areas you think might be problematic, and you don't sound like you are taking sides.

AVOID "WHY?" QUESTIONS

Asking "Why?" can cause problems in conflict interviews. "Why" asks for justification and tends to put people on the defensive. When people are upset and angry they already have a propensity to respond defensively. Mediators who ask "Why?" questions, especially when they ask a lot of them, can needlessly increase the emotional pitch of the interview.

Out of habit or laziness most of us ask "Why?" when we mean "What?". Perhaps we learned it during the "terrible two's" when we plagued our parents with, "Why?" "Why?" "Why?" However we picked up the habit, it can be a liability during a conflict interview.

EXAMPLE:

Poor: Why did you do that?

Better: What happened?

What was your objective in doing that?

EXAMPLE:

Poor:	Why are you always late?
Better:	What's the reason for your being late?
	You were late. What happened?

EXAMPLE:

Poor:	Why do you say that?
Better:	What's your thinking about that?
	What leads you to that conclusion?

It takes effort to break the "Why?" habit, but choosing our words well to ask the question we want answered is a skill, and it is important in conducting a good conflict interview. Instead of asking "Why...?" ask, "What happened?" or "What did he do?" or "What did she say?"

TECHNIQUE: SILENCE

We don't usually think of silence as an information-gathering tool. It seems like a contradiction. But, in fact, using silence skillfully can help you gather information in a conflict interview. There is something about silence that makes people uncomfortable, especially when they don't know one another well. People will usually break the silence with "small talk." It is not so much that they are interested in the small talk, it is that talking dispels the discomfort of silence.

EXAMPLE:

Betty:	[Silence]
Mediator:	Was it your account?
Betty:	Yeah. [Silence]
Mediator:	Did Bill's calling the customer bother you?
Betty:	Yeah. [Silence]
Mediator:	Do you think that it cost you the sale?
Betty:	Obviously![Silence]
Mediator:	Are you angry about losing the commission?
Betty:	Of course! Wouldn't you be? [Silence]

In this example the disputant says very little and is silent most of the time, which seems to make the mediator uncomfortable. As a result the mediator falls into the trap of talking more and more, using leading questions. It reminds me of a situation in which a boy who had committed a petty crime was supposed to meet with his probation officer twice a month. However, the boy was masterful at using silence. He made no statements voluntarily and answered the probation officer's questions with one word or a grunt. The boy's tactic paid off for him, because after two uncomfortable sessions the probation office told the boy that he didn't have to come to any more counseling sessions and that he only had to call in once a month.

As a mediator, you can use the discomfort of silence to the advantage of everyone concerned. When you are silent disputants feel uncomfortable and tend to talk more easily.

EXAMPLE:

Mediator: What happened?

Disputant: It was a serious crisis and everyone pitched in. A lot of people worked late everyday and came in on the weekends. We needed all the help we could get. There was a lot of team spirit and that was good. But Bill here was an exception. He left everyday at 5 o'clock. And when I asked him to help me out all he could say was, "It's not part of my job description." Can you believe it? Well, it just got to me. I've never been comfortable around him since then. I mean everyone except for Bill went the extra mile. And, well, I don't know..." [Disputant trails off].

Mediator: [Nodding] "Uh-huh." [Silence]

Disputant: Well, the director is always talking about being a team, and I believed him. But I don't want to be a team with Bill. Bill just isn't a team player.

WHEN TO USE SILENCE

Silence is used most effectively when the disputant has been on the topic and simply winds down. There is no reason for you to jump in immediately. Instead, remain silent for several seconds. Usually the disputant will go on with the story where he or she left off. Silence is best used in combination with active listening techniques, such as nodding  or saying "Uh huh" to communicate "Go on." On the other hand, if no one has spoken for a long while don't aggravate the discomfort by prolonging the silence.

Silence is not always effective and should be avoided in certain situations. Using silence with an openly hostile disputant is generally not a good idea. The discomfort caused by silence can add to the disputant's hostility rather than help communications.

TECHNIQUE: REVIEW AND SUM UP

The review and sum up is a summary of what the disputant has said, followed by a check-out. It functions like a mirror that you hold up to the disputant while asking whether it reflects how he or she sees the situation. The summary enhances understanding and promotes communication. You communicate to the disputants that you are attempting to understand each person's side of the story.

The review and sum up is a powerful technique with many uses. It signals how long to interview one disputant and when to move on to the next one's story, and it helps prepare the stage for mediation. If you are interrupted or get distracted you can get back on track with the review and sum up. Additionally, summarizing focuses the disputants' attention on the problem at hand and helps them to be more objective in their thinking about it.

HOW TO REVIEW

Briefly summarize the main points in the disputant's story, then ask, "*Is there anything else?*" "As you see it [point 1[+ [point 2] + [point 3].

Is there anything else?" As alternatives, you can follow your summary with, "Do I understand you correctly?" or "Do I have your story?"

The closed question, "Is there anything else?" following the summary elicits a yes/no answer. When you have gotten the points correctly, the disputant will usually answer with "No," or "That's about it" or "No, that's all." The negative response is what you are looking for. It tells you that you've gotten the disputant's story.

EXAMPLE:

Mediator: Okay, to summarize, Janet did not follow through on her promise to lay out your flyer. When you asked her about it she got angry and told other people that you were being sexist. Is there anything else?

Disputant: No, that's it. I'm really tired of her stories.

When you don't have all the information or are incorrect in your understanding, the disputant will answer, "Yes," to the question, "Is there anything else?" In most cases the disputant will then go on to correct you or say what else is bothering him or her. In those rare cases in which the disputant does not correct you, you can follow up with a probe such as, "What else happened today? or "What else is bothering you?"

EXAMPLE:

Mediator: Let me see if I understand how you see the situation. John and you each have assigned sales areas to work, but John has been calling people in your area. Recently, he took one of your major accounts to lunch and pitched him. Is there anything else?

Disputant: Yes! He didn't just pitch him. He gave him a lower quote than I did. It was a below-cost quote, too.

Mediator: Okay. So as you see it, you and John each
              have assigned sales areas. But John took one
              of your major accounts to lunch and
              pitched him with a below-cost quote that
              was lower than what you had quoted. Is
              there anything else?

Disputant: No, that's it. What John did was simply
              wrong.

It is vitally important that you follow the summary with "Is there anything else?" or one of the alternative questions. If you don't the disputant must be assertive and speak up to remind you of what you left out. "Wait a minute, you forgot...." or else the disputant may sit back and think, "I knew she wasn't listening. She doesn't care. Why bother?"

Don't worry about remembering everything the disputant said. Just focus on what seems to be the main issues. Suppose you forget something in your summary. If what you left out is important to the disputant he or she will usually tell you when you ask, "Is there anything else?" On the other hand, if you've forgotten something that is not particularly important to the disputant's story, when you ask, "Is there anything else?" the disputant is likely to answer, "That's about it. You've got it." You don't have to be right or remember everything, provided you use the review and sum up correctly.

If the disputant responds to your summary by saying, "Yes, there's more," use a probe such as, "What else happened today?" and continue interviewing until the disputant agrees with the summary. When the disputant agrees with your summary, say something like, "Good. I've heard your side. Now I'm going to talk to Sally." Then repeat the interviewing process with the next disputant.

You'll notice that the review and sum up begins with the phrase, "As you see it". This is important. Each time you review emphasize that this is "*your* story, not my story. This is how *you* see it. We're not talking about my perceptions or what is right or wrong. We're talking about how *you* see this conflict."

A SIGNAL

How the disputant responds to the review and sum up is a signal. The disputant's answer "No" not only indicates that you've gotten his or her story but that it is time to turn to the other disputant. On the other hand, the answer "Yes" to the question "Is there anything else?" indicates that you don't have the whole story or you've misunderstood the disputant, which is a signal to continue interviewing this disputant until you do get the whole story.

Both disputants answering "No" to the question, "Is there anything else?" is a signal that you have completed the information-gathering phase of conflict resolution and it is no time to move into mediation.

EXAMPLE:

Mediator: [Looking at first disputant] "As you see it, Bill is jumping to conclusions. Jeff, the owner of Abby Appliances, has been a friend of yours for years. Last week when you had lunch with Jeff you mentioned that your personal discount is practically cost. Jeff asked if you would buy for him on your discount as a favor and you agreed. You weren't invading his territory, you were just doing a favor for a friend. Is there anything else?

Disputant: No, that's the whole of it.

Mediator: [Turning toward Bill] As you see it, John took Jeff, who is one of your major accounts, to lunch and pitched him with a below cost quote which was lower than what you had quoted. Is there anything else?

Disputant: Yeah, you've got it.

When both disputants agree to your summary of their respective versions of the story it's your signal that the information-gathering phase is over. Both stories are laid out side-by-side for each to hear, and you are ready to move into mediation.

EXAMPLE:

Jake:	She tells me what to do constantly just as if I were a child or some incompetent. If I had a question, I'd ask. But I don't like being told what to do and how to do it all the time. And furthermore, it's none of her lousy business anyway! Tell her to stick her nose elsewhere and leave me alone. That's the problem. Isn't that enough?
Mediator:	As you see it, the problem is that she bosses you around. Is there anything else?

Here the mediator made an interpretation in the summary. The disputant did not actually say that the adversary bossed him around. It is easy to alter the disputant's words so that you've made an interpretation in the summary without checking it out first. Stick to the disputant's words when you summarize. Use a check-out to verify your interpretation before including them in the summary. Once again, when summarizing as when using the other techniques, go to the doing level. For example, the mediator could have said:

EXAMPLE:

Mediator:	The problem as you see it is that she tells you what to do when you haven't asked her to do so. Is there anything else?

In this review and sum up the mediator described the supervisor's behavior (the doing level) as the disputant presented it. By doing so, the mediator avoided the trap of inserting into the summary an interpretation that had not been affirmed by the disputant.

EXAMPLE:

David:	He reads my mail. Can you believe it? I mean, it's a federal offense! Oh, he denies it, but who would admit to such low behavior? He was on my phone, which he had no business using, and he found a personal letter on my desk and he read it. He actually took it out and read it! It's intolerable and disgusting and I want something done about it. I will not work with snoops!
Mediator:	As you see it, the problem is that he uses your phone and reads your mail. Is there anything else?

Here the mediator fell into the trap of generalizing. Disputants tend to generalize and exaggerate transgressions in order to build their case against the adversary. The mediator must avoid generalizing and summarize the specific doing instead. The easiest way to do this is to listen to the disputant's story while keeping in mind the question, "What did he or she do *today?*"

BETTER SUMMARY:

Mediator:	The problem as you see it is that he read a personal letter on your desk when he used your phone. Is there anything else?

ANOTHER EXAMPLE:

Randy:	She's the biggest nag I've ever met. The slightest little thing and she's complaining. If she would say her complaint in a civil tone, it would be one thing. But she whines. Today she started in again because I left a zip code off a form and I made an incorrect abbreviation. I've had it with her constant complaining.

Mediator:	The problem as you see it is that she corrected you when you left a zip code off a form and when you made an incorrect abbreviation. Is there anything else?

Here the mediator avoided the generalization trap. She didn't say, "She is always correcting you." And she translated loaded terms, like "nagged" and "whined" into neutral ones, like "corrected you" instead.

ANOTHER EXAMPLE:

Pat:	I can't depend on him for anything. Every time he does anything it is either wrong or late or both! I asked him to have something compiled by 3 p.m. today. Has he started on it? No, of course not! I'm tired of hounding him, and I'm not going to do it myself. Someone around here better come up with a solution, and it's not going to be me any more.
Mediator:	The problem as you see it is that his work is late and his work is incorrect. Is there anything else?

This is a little too general. Is all of this work always late and always incorrect? The disputant has exaggerated, and the mediator has generalized in the summary. The adversary is likely to resist this summary and become defensive. Always keep in mind the questions, "What is the problem *today?*" What is he or she *doing?* By focusing on these questions you can cut through to the core conflict. The problem today is that the disputant needed something completed by 3 pm and the adversary hasn't started on it yet. By keeping his eye on the ball, the mediator was able to bypass the issues of "I can't depend on him" and, "Everything he does is wrong".

Part of your agenda as the mediator is to simplify and bring the problem definition to a solvable situation. That something has to be completed by 3 p.m. today is solvable.

EXAMPLE:

> Better: The problem, as you see it, is that you asked
>   him to complete something by 3 pm today
>   and he hasn't started it yet. Is there any-
>   thing else?

Angry people tend to embroider and exaggerate their complaints. By keeping in mind the question "What is the problem *today?*" the mediator was able to cut through the exaggerations and attacks to get to what actually happened today.

The review and sum up acts like a mirror for the person telling the story. The disputant can step back and look at the problem more objectively. When judgmental words are removed and the problem is translated to the doing level, the conflicts goes from an insolvable crisis to a solvable disagreement. Suddenly the problem doesn't look so bad. Simultaneously, the adversary hears the problem concisely stated— sometimes for the first time.

REVIEW AND SUM UP OFTEN

Don't let the disputant go on and on. Frequent summarizing may sound redundant, but it helps you to control the process. Every time you think you have the story, review and sum up. When you get stuck or confused and don't know what to do, review and sum up. "As you see it.... Is there anything else?" The disputant goes on with the story. "Yes, there's more." "What is the problem, as you see it?" "Well, this guy...." You're back on track again. As soon as you think you understand the story, review and sum up again.

Rule of Thumb: When in doubt, review and sum up.

OTHER USES OF REVIEW AND SUM UP

The dispute interview is not a social conversation in which you are expected to wait politely for a break in the disputant's stream of words before speaking. If the disputant wanders from the problem being discussed, cut him or her off. The easiest way to do this is with the review and sum up. Interrupt with, "So as you see it, the problem is...." Summarize what the disputant has said on the topic, then ask, "Is there anything else?" or follow with a probe such as, "What else happened?" or "What else is bothersome *today?*"

In this way you maintain control by pulling the disputant back to the topic at the same time that you demonstrate your desire to understand the disputant by the use of the summary. Even though you may have had to interrupt the disputant, he or she will probably not see the interruption as rude when the mediator summarizes the complaint.

When You've Been Interrupted

The review and sum up technique is helpful for getting back on track after an interruption. Here's how: Review and sum up what you remember of the story and ask, "Is there anything else?" Alternatively, you can follow the summary with a probe such as, "And what else happened?" or "What else is bothering you?"

When You've Been Distracted

Sometimes you'll get distracted and realize you haven't heard what the person said. You can recoup with the review and sum up. "Let's see if I have it. As you see it, when John.... Is there anything else?" Even when you heard only a portion of the story you won't lose rapport because by using the review and sum up you communicate, "I want to hear you."

Taking Notes

 Note taking can pose problems. Disputants wonder what you are writing and what you will do with it, and they tend to clam up. Another problem is that while you're writing, you miss subtleties and may not hear all that the disputant says. And it is easier to lose control when taking notes because your attention is not fully on the disputants, which makes it easier for them to begin bickering.

The more you use the review and sum up, the better you'll get at it and the easier it will be to remember the disputants' stories. Try this trick. When you hear a main point, touch one of your fingers, as if you were counting. When you hear the second major point, touch your second finger and so forth until have all the points. As you summarize, touch each finger. I don't know why but it helps many people to remember the points.

When you review frequently, the repetition will help you remember the points. Don't worry if you don't get all the points into the summary. The disputant will correct you—provided you ask, "Is there anything else?" And don't worry about being right. Just use the technique right and you'll be okay.

If you do decide to take notes, do it in conjunction with the review and sum up. After the disputant has agreed to the accuracy of your summary, stop and write down the points in the summary. Here you're not taking your attention away from the disputant's story. And you can feel confident that your summary is accurate, since the disputant has just verified it. Now the disputants know what you are writing, which will reduce their suspicions. It's a good idea to explain to the disputants what you will do with the notes.

REVIEWING SETS THE STAGE FOR MEDIATION

When each disputant has agreed with your summary of his or her story, then quickly summarize each disputant's story, one after another. Only this time don't follow the summary with "Is there anything else?" The objects is to have each story on the table, ready for mediation. "Joe, as you see it.... And Robert, as you see the situation...."

PUTTING IT ALL TOGETHER

Let's return to Alice, the City Administrator who tried to intervene in the conflict between Jeff, the Recycle Deputy and Sheila, the Administrative Assistant. As the Coach, I will help Alice keep on track.

EXAMPLE

Coach:	*Okay, Alice, begin by laying the ground rules.*
Alice:	I called the two of you together to find out what's been going on. [Looking at Sheila] "I will listen to Sheila's side first. [Looking at Jeff] Then I want to hear how Jeff sees the problem. [Looking at Sheila] Sheila, what is the problem as you see it? (laying the ground rules; probe)
Sheila:	Jeff's been dumping his work on me.
Jeff:	I have not! What a bunch of....
Alice:	[Raising her hand towards Jeff] Hold on, I'll hear your story next. Llooking at Sheila] Dumping work on you? (reestablishing control with a hand gesture while repeating the ground rules; repeat)
Coach:	*Good, Alice, you didn't let Jeff break in.*
Sheila:	He thinks that since he's a Deputy that he doesn't have to do paperwork.
Alice:	Really! [Turning towards Jeff] You know you are expected to do your own paper work. Why are you....
Coach:	*Hold on a minute, Alice. You are lecturing Jeff and asking him to answer to Sheila's story. It sounds like you're taking sides. Just find out how Sheila sees the problem. Begin again with a probe.*
Alice:	What happened? (probe)
Sheila:	Well, this morning I found this note on my desk that said, "Here's a mock-up for the flyer. I need it by Wednesday." Can you believe it! I am *not* his secretary!
Alice:	Do you mean that you think he expected you to put together his Recycling Contest flyer? (specific check-out)

Sheila:	Exactly. Well, I am *not* doing it.
Alice:	I can understand that. We're all supposed to do our own paperwork around here.
Coach:	*Wait, Alice. You're agreeing with Sheila. This is going to get you into trouble. You'll lose your impartiality. Use a probe to get to the facts of the problem.*
Alice:	Uh, what happened? (probe)
Sheila:	Well, I put it back on his desk and told him I wasn't doing it. I was very nice about it— considering the way he treats me.
Jeff;	The hell she was!
Alice:	[Raising her hand towards Jeff, then looking at Sheila] Has Jeff asked you to do other things? Like the data sheets? Or the log book? (maintaining control with hand gesture)
Sheila:	Well, uh, yeah. Yes! Last week he wanted me to print out his data sheets. It's ridiculous. I am *not* his secretary.
Coach:	*What's happening here? Who brought up the data sheets?*
Alice:	I guess I did.
Coach:	*Yes, you asked a leading question. Don't lead Sheila into other areas. Just find out how she sees the problem. You've gotten distracted now, so sum up and see what happens.*
Alice:	As you see it, Jeff left a note asking you to lay out a flyer for the Recycling Contest. You told him you weren't going to do the flyer, and you put the note back on his desk. Is there anything else? (review and sum up)
Sheila:	Yeah, I don't see where he gets off treating me like a second-class citizen.
Alice:	Second class citizen? (repeat)

Sheila: Yes, he's so rude.

Alice: Rude? What did he do? (repeat, probe)

Sheila: Well, last year when I moved over here from the Central Office is when it all started. He was rude then and he's still rude.

Alice: What did he do *today?* (probe focused on here-and-now)

Sheila: He acts like he thinks he's something special just because he's a Deputy.

Alice: Something special? (repeat)

Sheila: Yeah, he's stuck up!

Alice: I'm stuck. What do I do now?

Coach: *Sheila is using a lot of loaded words like, rude, second-class citizen, stuck up. Sounds like a lot of feelings are there. How do you suppose she feels?*

Alice: I don't know. I suppose she feels she's being treated inferiorly, or being left out.

Coach: *Good, try that out on her with a feeling check-out.*

Alice: Do you mean that you feel left out? (feeling check-out)

Sheila: Well, not exactly left out. It's uh....

Alice: Uh-huh. (silence and active listening)

Sheila: Uh....

Alice: Go on. (active listening)

Sheila: I mean he doesn't even give me the time of day—or even say "Hello" in the morning.

Alice: Do you mean that he doesn't greet you when he comes in? (general check-out)

Sheila: Yeah, I don't like the guy any more than he likes me. But he could be polite, couldn't he? It's really offensive to be treated like an office fixture.

Alice:	Do you mean that when he doesn't say, "Hello" you are offended because you feel like an office fixture? (feeling check-out)
Sheila:	Yeah, how would you feel?
Alice:	Well, I would feel....
Coach:	*Don't answer that. You'll sound like you're taking sides.*
Alice:	Do you mean you feel ignored? (feeling check-out)
Sheila:	Yet, he treats me like I'm nothing—a piece of furniture—except, of course, when he wants something.
Alice:	Let's see if I understand, Sheila. As you see it, Jeff left a note asking you to put together a flier. Since it's not part of your job you put it back on his desk and told him you were not going to do it. Also, Jeff doesn't say "Hello" to you when he comes in. It's impolite and you feel ignored. Is there anything else? (reveiw and sum up)
Sheila:	No. That's it.
Alice:	[Turning to Jeff] Okay, Jeff, what's this about making Sheila do your work.
Jeff:	Oh, Christ! I couldn't *make* that turkey do anything.
Sheila:	See! See how he treats me! I refuse to....
Alice:	[Raising a hand toward Sheila] Hold on. Hold on. I heard your side. [Looking at Jeff] That's no way to talk about Sheila.
Jeff:	You're not interested in what I have to say. What's the point of this?
Coach:	*What's going on here, Alice?*
Alice:	Jeff is definitely upset.
Coach:	*How did that happen? What did* ***you*** *do?*
Alice:	I got on his case for calling Sheila a turkey.

Coach: *Yes, and you began by asking Jeff to answer to*
            Sheila's story. The objective now is to find out
            how Jeff sees the problem. Begin again.

Alice: Jeff, what's your side? How do you see the
            problem? (probe)

Jeff: Last week Sheila was bragging to me
            about....

Sheila: I was not! I was....

Alice: [Looking at Sheila and raising her hand]
            Sheila, I heard your side. I'm listening to
            Jeff's side now. (restating the ground rules,
            escalating force to regain control) Jeff, go
            on.

Jeff: She was telling me about a course she took
            in desktop publishing and how she learned
            how to lay out professional-looking flyers.
            So I asked her if she would help me with the
            Recycling Contest flyer, and she said she
            would.

Sheila: I never....

Alice: [Holding up her hand] Hold on. (using
            hand gesture for control)

Jeff: So I put the mock-up of the flyer on her
            desk. And she goes berserk. From the way
            she acted, you'd think I was the worst
            person in the world.

Sheila: You are, t-u-r-k-e-y!

Alice: [Holding up her hand toward Sheila, then
            looking at Jeff] Do you mean you thought
            Sheila said she would put the flyer to-
            gether?" (using hand gesture for control,
            check-out)

Jeff: Well, yeah. She knows how to do it. She
            made sure to let me know that! And she said
            she would help. What would you think?

Alice: Well, I would...uh.... Do you mean you're
             confused? (feeling check-out)
Coach: *Good, Alice, you caught yourself.*
Jeff: Yeah, that's for sure. She said she would
             help, and then when I took her up on her
             offer she goes ballistic.
Alice: Ballistic? (repeat)
Jeff: Well, you see how she's acting and what
             she's saying, don't you?
Alice: What do you mean? (probe)
Jeff: I mean she over-reacts to the max.
Alice: What did she do? (probe)
Jeff: She stomps around and yells. She was
             yelling so loud when I was on the phone. I
             was really embarrassed.
Alice: Do you mean that you think her reaction
             was unjustified? (general check-out)
Jeff: Yeah. That's putting it mildly!
Alice: So as you see it, Sheila said she would help
             you with the flyer, but when you left the
             mock-up on her desk she refused and got
             angry. Is there anything else? (review and
             sum up)
Jeff: Yeah, these excessive attacks on me are
             childish and uncalled for. What's her prob-
             lem? PMS or something!
Alice: Really, Jeff, what a thing to say!
Jeff: Oh, what's the use!
Alice: Uh, do you mean you're upset by her angry
             comments? (feeling check-out)
Coach: *Good, you got back on track.*
Jeff: Well, I definitely don't like her nasty tongue.
             But I can take it. What I mean is that I don't
             see why Sheila should be allowed to get away
             with throwing tantrums. This is suppose to
             be a professional office.

Alice: Do you mean that you think the way Sheila
                expresses her anger is not business-like?
                (general check-out, defuses loaded words)
Jeff: Exactly. What do *you* think?
Alice: Well, I...uh....
Coach: *Don't answer that question. Review Jeff's side*
                instead.
Alice: Let's see if I've got it. As you see it, Sheila
                said she would help you with your flyer, but
                when you left the mock-up on her desk she
                got angry and refused to help. You think
                that the way she acts when she's angry is
                unbusiness-like. Is there anything else?
                (review and sum up)
Jeff: That's it.
Coach: *Good. Now sum up both stories again, and*
                you're ready to move into mediation.
Alice: [Looking at Sheila] As you see it, Jeff left a
                note asking you to put together a flyer,
                which is not part of your job, so you put it
                back on his desk and told him you were not
                going to do it. Plus Jeff doesn't say "Hello"
                to you when he comes in, which makes you
                feel ignored. [Looking at Jeff] And the way
                you see it, Sheila said she would help you
                with your flyer but then refused to help and
                got angry when you left the mock-up on her
                desk. You think that the way she acts when
                she's angry is unbusiness-like. (review and
                sum up)

How does this second interview compare with Alice's first one (see
page 7)? Alice kept the interview under control. She didn't get sucked
into arguing. And she avoided getting sidetracked into an old disagreement with Jeff. In short, Alice started off well and maximized the

possibility that Sheila and Jeff will come up with a workable arrangement. She communicated, "I expect you to solve your problems. I am not going to take sides."

EXAMPLE:

Father:	[Pointing to the chair to his left] Mickey, sit here. [Gesturing toward chair on his right] Sally, over here. I asked the two of you to meet me here in my den so that we could discuss this situation with the phone and come up with a solution." (arranged the setting, took control)
Sally:	What situation? The phone is....
Father:	Hold on. First I'm going to describe how we're going to do this. Then we'll get into the phone.
Coach:	*Good, Dad, you kept control. Go on.*
Father:	I want to understand how each of you sees the situation. I'll talk to you one at a time, beginning with Mickey. Then I'll hear your side, Sally. (set ground rules) Mickey, what's the situation as you see it?
Mickey:	She's a bully—she thinks she owns the phone.
Father:	Owns the phone? (repeat)
Mickey:	Yeah, she's on it all the time. And because of her I missed Little League practice. And it isn't fair. You don't think it's fair, do you, Dad?
Father:	No, it's not fair, Mickey. Little League is important.
Sally:	Oh, Gawd! Give me a break, will you! Look what the big bad sister did this time!
Father:	Don't you get sassy. Little League builds character and confidence. You have no business....

Coach: *Hold on. What happened, Dad?*
Father: Sally is talking back again.
Coach: *When you agreed with Mickey you took his side and lost your impartiality.*
Father: I see what you mean.
Coach: *Use a review to get back on track.*
Father: You said that because Sally was on the phone you missed Little League. What happened? (probe)
Mickey: The Coach said that he would call with the time of the special practice session. I didn't get his call because she....[Mickey turns toward Sally while grimacing] she was hogging the phone—again!
Father: [Tapping his chest] Talk to me, Mickey. (redirecting disputant's attention to mediator)
Coach: *Good.*
Father: Do you mean that the line was busy and the coach couldn't get through? (specifc checkout)
Mickey: That's right! So I missed the practice. It didn't look good, especially right before the big game.
Father: Uh-huh, so you were waiting for a call from the coach with the time for the practice, but the line was busy because Sally was on the phone. As a result you missed the practice. Is there anything else? (review and sum up)
Mickey: Naw.
Father: [Turning to Sally] Now I want to hear your side. Why were you hogging the phone?
Sally: What a crock! You're not interested in my side. And I wasn't hogging the phone!
Father: How do *you* see it? What happened? (probe)

Coach:	*Good. You asked Sally to answer to Mickey's story, which set her off. But you got back on track by refocusing on Sally's concerns.*
Sally:	He said that the coach was going to call and I couldn't use the phone until he did. Well, I waited two hours and then I had an important call.
Mickey:	What was so important? Ask her! It was that idiot she calls a boyfriend.
Sally:	Shut your mouth, ape breath!
Father:	Hold on. [Waving a plam down hand at Mickey. "I heard your side. (maintaining control with hand gesture) [Turning to Sally] What happened? (probe)
Coach:	*You got them back under control. Good.*
Sally:	He acted like a total jerk.
Father:	Like a jerk? What did he do? (repeat, probe)
Sally:	He was being a brat.
Father:	What happened? (probe)
Sally:	He kept yelling at me to get off. And when I didn't, he hung up the phone on me. He was completely out of line.
Father:	Let me see if I understand. You stayed off the phone for two hours until you got an important call. Mickey told you to get off and then hung up the phone while you were still talking. Is there anything else? (review and sum up)
Sally:	Yeah. I don't think Little League is so important, but because Mickey asked me I stayed off the phone. But when I was on an important call, he yells in the background and hangs up on my call. Things are important to me, too. He's not the only one around here.

Father:	Do you mean you feel he doesn't appreciate your staying off the phone two hours? (feeling check-out)
Sally:	Yeah, why should I do anything for the jerk? Then he hangs up my call. That call was important!
Mickey:	What was so important, lame brain?
Father:	Hold on, Mickey." [To Sally] "Do you mean you feel he doesn't respect what's important to you? (maintaining control, feeling check-out)
Sally:	You've got it. Just listen to him.
Father:	So you stayed off the phone for two hours because it was important to Mickey, but when you got an important call, he hung up your call. Is there anything else? (review and sum up)
Sally:	That's pretty much it. I can't deal with him.
Coach:	*Good. Now summarize both stories quickly, and the stage is set for mediation.*
Father:	[To Mickey] You were waiting for the coach to call about practice, and you asked Sally to stay off the phone. But Sally got on the phone, and as a result you missed the call and the practice. [Turning to Sally] Because it was important to Mickey you stayed off the phone for two hours, but he did not reciprocate and he hung up on your important call. (review and sum up)

Remaining impartial is particularly challenging when the mediator is a family member. It is vital always to keep in mind that as the mediator you are not going to come up with a solution. You don't have to decide who the good guy is. You don't have to determine where reality lies, or who is right and who is wrong. All you have to do is to get the disputants to state their stories which you then summarize back to them. It doesn't matter who is right and who is wrong. It is tempting to affix blame, but your objective in the conflict interview is to find out how each disputant sees the situation.

REVIEW OF PRINCIPLES

In the following examples, the mediator will violate one or more of the principles or do's and don'ts of using the techniques just discussed. In each case, see if you can determine what error the Poor Mediator made and what a Better Mediator would do or say differently.

REVIEW 1:

John:	Mary says he's got a problem with authority.
Poor:	Problem with authority?

The mediator didn't find out how John sees the situation. Instead, he allowed John to say how he thinks Mary sees the problem. We don't know who Mary is. Mary is some other person somewhere else. We want to know how John sees the problem. If Mary is a party to the dispute, then she should participate in the mediation.

Better:	What is the problem as *you* see it?

The Better Mediator ignored John's speculations about how Mary sees things and refocused attention to John's opinion of what is going on.

REVIEW 2:

Susan:	When I first transferred here she was really unfriendly to me.
Poor:	What did she *do?*

Here, the disputant is going into past events. Who cares what happened when she first came here? The past can't be changed. We care about what is occurring in the "now" because conflicts are resolved in the here-and-now.

Better: What is the problem *today?*

The Better Mediator ignored Susan's resentment from the past and redirected her attention to what was happening today. Current situations can be mediated.

REVIEW 3:

Ralph: Do you know what he did last year?
Poor: What did he *do?*

The Poor Mediator made a mistake similar to that of the previous example. We don't want to know what happened last year. We can't mediate the past. We want to know what caused the conflict today so that we can mediate what the disputants will do in the future.

Better: What did he do *today?*

This question is simple but excellent. It is an open question or a probe that puts pressure on the disputant to elaborate because it can't be answered with a "yes" or a "no". It focuses on the doing level in the here and now where problems can be solved.

REVIEW 4:

Mediator: What's the problem as you see it?
Beth: I was making a doctor appointment for a personal health matter when I heard clicking on the phone. He was in his room, and he has an extension in there. Of course, I thought it was him. Who else could it be? What would you think?
Poor: Yeah, It's pretty understandable. I can see how you could get that impression.
Bob: You two can agree all you want, but I don't think it's understandable at all! And I really fail to see what I've got to gain by listening to this.

The Poor Mediator lost impartiality by emphathizing with Beth. Disputants will often try to get the mediator to side with them. Generally, this is done by asking the mediator questions, such as "Well how would *you* feel?" or, "What would *you* do?" Answering such questions is a trap.

It is better if the mediator ignores the question completely and asks the disputant, "What did he do?" But it is awfully hard not to answer the disputant's questions because we've been trained that nice, polite people respond to questions. It is impolite to ignore questions. In polite society people criticize us when we respond to a question with a question. But being polite is not your objective in conflict resolution. You are not trying to be the disputant's pal.

Whether disputant mean to or not, their questions are usually sabbotaging. As a mediator, you should stay far away from disputants' questions. As soon as you say how you feel or what you would do, you've lost your impartiality.

EXAMPLE:

Beth:	Well, what do *you* think I should do?
Poor:	What I think is not important to this discussion.
Beth:	It certainly is important. I mean, I'd like to know just how you expect me to put up with this bull. Just what would *you* do with his snooping?

If the disputant asks a question, don't give a lecture. Then the disputant can argue with you and you'll get sidetracked into your own conflict with the disputant. Instead, make no response to the disputant's question and proceed with gathering information.

BETTER EXAMPLE:

Beth:	I was making a doctor's appointment for a health matter when I heard clicking on the

	phone. He was in his room, and he has an extension in there. Of course, I thought it was him. Who else could it be? What would *you* think?
Better:	Let me see if I understand. You were making a doctor appointment, and when you heard clicking on the line you thought Bob was listening in on your call from his room. Is there anything else?
Beth:	Yeah, that's it alright. It's incredible!

The review and sum up technique is a wonderful tool for sidestepping these traps. Ignore the disputant's questions and review and sum up instead. It builds rapport with the disputant because you demonstrate that you're trying to understand. At the same time, you communicate impartiality to the adversary because you've stated the "facts M'am, just the fact." And you've maintained control. That is a lot to accomplish with one technique!

REVIEW 5:

Jeff:	I tried to be friendly and got him a cup of coffee and he just snarled and walked out of the room.
Poor:	The problem as you see it is that he snarled at you when you got him a cup of coffee. Is there anything else?

The word "snarled" is loaded and likely to antagonize the adversary when he hears it. Part of the mediator's role is to defuse the conflict, and this can be accomplished by substituting more neutral language for the loaded words disputants use. Here, for example, the mediator might have used "looked annoyed" instead of "snarled."

On the other hand, focusing on the annoyed reaction may be missing the real issue—the underlying hurt that Jeff experienced. The mediator could have reached this with a feeling check.

BETTER EXAMPLE:

Jeff: I tried to be friendly and got him a cup of coffee and he just snarled and walked out of the room.

Mediator: Do you mean you felt unappreciated?

Jeff: Yeah, I mean he could have at least acknowledged it, but he just walked out of the room.

Mediator: The problem as you see it is that you got him a cup of coffee but he just walked out of the room without acknowledging your friendly gesture. Is there anything else?

Jeff: No! I'd say that that was quite enough.

The Better Mediator used the check-out to draw out the disputant's feelings behind the content. Then he reviewed and summed up the disputant's complaint on the doing level.

REVIEW 6:

Mediator: The problem as you see it is that you and Linda ate lunch together until Trudy got Linda interested in healthy eating and exercising. Since then you've been eating alone. Is there anything else?

Judith: Yeah. Linda and I used to eat lunch together until that Trudy came along with all of her health food and exercise baloney. Pretty soon I couldn't eat anything. Chips are bad. Ham sandwiches are bad. Smart drinks are good. Mega-this and mega-that. Now she's talking caloric restriction—whatever *that* is—and she's got Linda jogging instead of eating. So I eat alone and avoid the daily sermon.

Mediator: The problem as you see it is that you and

	Linda used to eat lunch together. Now Linda and Trudy jog during lunch and you eat alone. Is there anything else?
Judith:	Yeah, I mean, Linda and I used to eat to- gether, but now all that seems to matter is this stupid health kick. You know, I get really sick and tired of hearing it.

When you seem to understand the disputant's view, and summarize a number of times but the disputant keeps rejecting the summary without adding anything more, there could be underlying hurt feelings. Here, it might be appropriate to go to the feeling level.

BETTER EXAMPLE:

Mediator:	Do you mean you feel excluded and now you must eat alone?
Judith:	Of course, I really don't *care* what they do but I think Trudy blabs on about the health food stuff just to push me out! It's rude and it's unfriendly.
Mediator:	Let's see if I have it. The problem as you see it is that you used to enjoy having lunch with Linda. But when Trudy came along she interested Linda in health foods and exercising. You feel excluded since you have little interest in health foods, so you now eat alone. Is there anything else?
Judith:	No, that basically it.

The rule of thumb is to go after the doing level first, and if the disputant doesn't agree with the summary after a few attempts, switch your focus to the feeling level. The feeling level is important, but it is not the primary target in conflict resolution in the workplace or playground.

REVIEW 7:

> Joan: [Coming into your office and closing the door] I've just got to talk with your about this problem with Mary.
>
> Poor: What did she do?

The mediator has communicated that when there is a problem around here it should be taken to the boss—King Solomon. By even listening to the story, the mediator has become involved. Furthermore, the mediator has communicated that the way we solve problems around here is to go to the authority.

Some people's style is to go to the boss with complaints about other people. Often they have a hidden agenda which is to turn the boss against the adversary. When the adversary hears about it, then he or she will pull you aside to tell you the sins of the first person. Before you know it, you've been pulled into the old mother/father routine, in which the child plays the mother against the father.

BETTER EXAMPLE:

> Mediator: [Cutting him off] William, I'm glad you've brought this situation out. Before you go into it, I think it would be a good idea if I called Mary in so that we can find out what's going on and clear things up.

By refusing to listen to the problem behind closed doors, and by calling in the other party, you have stopped the problem of getting pulled into the middle. When you insist on having both disputants present, you communicate the message that around here people deal openly with problems and work toward solutions.

Sometimes people will adamantly refuse to meet with the adversary because they say they can't stand confrontation. Instead, they plead to talk alone with you, the boss—or teacher, coach, co-worker. This is a common style of handling conflict, and it generally works for a lot of people. They get a lot of people on their side and they poison people's opinions of the adversary. You can see how this can get out of hand and create a tense situation. However, if you are firm in you insistence that the other party be present, the disputant can refuse only up to a point. Beyond that, the person begins to look like the troublemaker.

EXAMPLE:

> Mediator: I've brought the two of you together so that
>   we can get to the bottom of things. Bill,
>   what would you like to discuss?
> Bill: Nothing.

Without the adversary present, Bill can rant and rave about the adversary. He can tell you how bad the other person is without risking repercussions. Bill has the upper hand because his adversary doesn't know about the meeting or what was said, which allows Bill to poison the boss or teacher's opinion and slink out. So it isn't too surprising that Bill might be less willing to express his complaint with the adversary present.

EXAMPLE:

> Mediator: I brought the two of you together because
>   there seems to be some difficulty between
>   you and it has been bothering Bill. Bill, what
>   is the problem as *you* see it?

Of course, Bill will still be reluctant to discuss his conflict openly, but it is harder to rebuff the question, "What is the problem as you see it?" than it is to the question answer "nothing" to the question "What do you want to discuss?"

REVIEW 8:

> Disputant: He just has a condescending attitude and he
> thinks he's better than me. Well, he's not!
> Mediator: What did he do today?
> Disputant: He's always bragging
> about the opera he
> went to and about
> important people he
> knows. He thinks he's
> superior. He thinks
> he's more cultured than
> me. Well, he's nothing!

As the mediator, ask yourself, "What is this guy doing on the doing level?" He's bragging. But bragging is loaded. What is he *doing?* What is the doing of bragging? Bragging is talking. What is he talking about? He's talking about the opera and important people. From this, the mediator can formulate a review and sum up.

EXAMPLE:

> Mediator: The problem as you see it is that he's talked
> about the opera and the important people
> he knows. Is there anything else?
> Disputant: Yeah! He thinks he's such a big deal. But he
> is nothing!

The mediator has given a good review of what the disputant said, but the disputant has rejected the summary. The mediator might ask him or herself, "What is going one here? How does this person feel about the guy talking about opera and important people? Maybe the disputant feels that this guy is trying to seem superior." From this the mediator can formulate a feeling check-out.

BETTER EXAMPLE:

Mediator: Do you mean you think he acts as if he
            thinks he is superior to you?

Disputant: That's right. He's always putting on airs and
            acting like he's better than me, but he's no
            better!

REVIEW 9:

Disputant: Jack claims he can't type, and he gets others
            to do his typing, and he takes long breaks,
            which he's not supposed to do. Then I have
            to cover for him. I'm getting tired of watch-
            ing him getting paid for pretending to work.
            He gets more than me, too. I work for my
            pay check. I'm sick of this freeloader. I
            want him to shape up now!

What is Jack *doing* that is bugging the disputant? He is not doing
his work? Which work? He is not typing? He is getting other people to
do his typing. What else? He takes unapproved breaks and the disputant
has to cover for him. He also gets paid more than the disputant. Pay is
not something that can be mediated so leave it out of the summary—at
least in the first stab.

BETTER EXAMPLE:

Mediator: The problem as you see it is that Jack gets
            other people to do his typing and you have
            to cover for him when he's on break. Is
            there anything else?

Huge problems can be made into small manageable problems.
Angry people exaggerate and embroider the problem to match their
emotional state. That's the nature of what people do. As the mediator,
you have to cut through that. This is especially important when the

disputant is accusing the adversary of being "a rip-off artist" or "inconsiderate" or "manipulating," and so forth. These kinds of things can't be mediated.

Furthermore, as the adversary listens to being called a "freeloader" or "lazy", for example, he or she is probably getting angrier and angrier and will probably get more and more defensive—all of which makes mediating a good action plan very difficult. Part of your job as the mediator is to gather information and keep it in perspective by bringing it back down to a realistic statement of what is going on *today* at the *doing level.* You will have the problem half-solved by the time you get the interview done—*by making it more solvable.* The disputants make the problem unsolvable. You know that when you are angry, chances are you would want to show the mediator that the situation is unsolvable and it is the other person's fault, which is why you are so frustrated.

CHAPTER 4

DECISION POINT

*A*ll the disputants agreeing with your review and sum up of their respective view points is a signal that you have completed information-gathering, which brings you to a decision point.

OPTIONS

Do nothing
Give a directive
Transfer
Refer
Mediate
Terminate

DO NOTHING

On the face of it, doing nothing might not seem like an option. But remember that the interview is a significant part of conflict resolution. Sometimes getting the dispute out into the open and clarifying disputants' complaints clears up misunderstandings. "You mean that's what you were thinking when you did that?"

GIVE A DIRECTIVE

Another option is for you to direct disputants to act in a particular way in the future. There is always a temptation to take this option. But remember that when you tell people what to do you've stepped into the shoes of King Solomon, and by doing so you take on responsibility for the resolution. Furthermore, you convey the message that you will issue edicts and rulings like a judge. Generally, you should exercise this option only after mediation has failed.

TRANSFER

A solution might be to move one or both disputants to another location or department. If you are a teacher this may be moving a student into another classroom, for example, or reassigning seats so that students will have less contact with one another. Again, transfer is generally an option to be considered after failed mediation.

REFER

The referral option involves sending one or both disputants to a specialist, such as a mental health worker or a lawyer. This may be a suggestion that disputants can take or reject, or it may be combined with the giving directive option in which disputants are required to go to the specialist.

Referral might be the appropriate option when certain things are uncovered during the interview that suggest the problem needs specialized attention. Specialized problems might be medical conditions, legal issues, financial concerns, behavioral problems, or psychological issues. If a specialized problem is revealed to be at the core of the dispute, it is best for you to bow out and refer the disputant to a specialist. For example, you can't mediate a medical problem. If there is a legal issue, such as whether or not a disputant has violated someone's civil rights, for example, it is best for you to get an attorney or other expert specialist involved. Don't try to mediate these sort of things. You may be doing the disputants a disservice, and you may be taking on some sort of liability.

TERMINATE

If you have formal authority, such as being a supervisor, you may have the power to terminate one or both disputants. If you're a teacher in an educational setting and the disputants are students, the termination option would be to expel. In membership groups such as a professional association, it might be to discontinue membership.

Exercising the termination option should be considered as a last resort. Termination should not be done lightly. It can be tramatic for the disputants which could lead to legal difficulties vis-a-vis employment contracts, for example. On the other hand there are situations when termination is the appropriate decision. In the workplace this might be when there is a chronic behavioral problem interfering with productivity despite other options having been exhausted and the disputant having received documented warnings.

The termination option is probably exercised most often in secondary school situations in which a disputant has a history of physical fighting or drug use, for example. In the workplace it might be when the person has engaged in repeated sexual harassment. For the most part, however, termination should be considered only after other options have been exhausted.

CHAPTER 5

MEDIATION

Generally, the first recommended option is mediation. If it fails, then consider other options. The purpose of mediation is to help the disputants resolve their dispute while simultaneously teaching them how to solve future problems.

GOAL OF MEDIATION?

Up to this point you have been gathering information on the nature and scope of the dispute. Your *objective in the mediation phase of conflict resolution is to help the disputants develop a mutually agreeable action plan.* The emphasis here is on mutually agreeable. Obviously, if they both don't agree to it, the plan will have a slim chance of working.

Secondary objectives are to reduce hostility between the disputants, to reduce the frequency of actions that interfere with productivity and harmony in the workplace or in the setting where the disputants interact, and to teach disputants tools for resolving future disagreements.

NOT A PANACEA

Not every attempt to mediate is going to work, and not every dispute can be mediated. There are certain situations in which people are entrenched in their positions which makes compromise difficult. But, in general, mediation is worth a try. Even if a full resolution is not reached you may get agreement on a smaller point, which represents progress. In fact, it's not realistic to expect that a one-time mediation is going to resolve a deep-seated conflict, especially if it is one of long duration. Conflict resolution is more of a shaping process in which disputants make incremental compromises. As each step toward better interaction works, disputants become more motivated and more skillful at negotiating agreements before disagreements reach the level of "dispute."

COMPROMISE

The mediated resolution is almost always a compromise in which each disputant agrees to do something more to the liking of the other. However, the compromise will not always be a 50-50, equal agreement. From your point of view, one side may give more than the other. But your opinion should stay out of it. You may not understand the weight that a person's compromise means to him or her. To you, the compromise may seem like a small thing, but to the person it may represent a sginificant concession. When the resolutions seems to be one disputant giving more than the other, keep in mind that it is the *disputants' agreement.* It is not for you to pass judgment on who should be giving more, or who is getting the better deal.

MUTUALLY AGREEABLE

The critical thing about the resolution is not a 50-50 compromise, but that the plan is *agreeable to all disputants.* There could be a wonderfully balanced plan in which each disputant gave equally. But if there is no consensus on the plan and the disputants don't mutually agree to it, little likelihood exists that it will work to lessen the conflict.

HOW TO MEDIATE

The information-gathering phase ends when disputants have affirmed your review and sum up. The mediation phase begins by making a concise summary of each disputant's side. In the introductory summary you don't ask, "Is there anything else?" Instead, start mediation with a summary of each disputant's story, one after another—in something of an overview fashion. For example, "As you see it...". You move immediately to the next disputant and summarize his or her story, "As you see it...". If there are more than two disputants, you continue with one story after another, until you have summarized all the sides of the dispute. The purpose of the introductory summary is to lay out all the disputants' stories.

ELICIT SUGGESTIONS

After all sides of the dispute have been clearly summarized, elicit a suggestion for resolving the dispute. *Elicit means to call out from or otherwise to get the disputants to make suggestions.* Never make suggestions yourself. This will be very hard to resist. If you fall into the trap of making suggestions, mediation tends to fall apart. Ironically, your making suggestions can lead to losing control.

EXAMPLE:

Mediator:	What do you suggest?
Larry:	Important calls come for me when I'm not here and I never hear about them. It's a drag and causes me a lot of trouble.
Mediator:	You could put a message pad by the phone.
Larry:	Yeah, but she wouldn't use it.
Mediator:	You could get your own phone.
Larry:	Yeah, but I can't afford it.
Mediator:	You could try voice mail with a personal extension.
Larry:	Naw, my friends don't like recorded messages.
Mediator:	You could explain how important it is to you.
Larry:	Naw, she doesn't care what I think.

A common trap is falling into the "yes, but" routine. Here you make a suggestion only to have it dismissed with, "Yes, but I tried that and it didn't work because she wouldn't...". Each suggestion, no matter how practical or workable is quickly shown to be unworkable: "Yes, but that would work because I don't have enough money...." or "They wouldn't allow it...." or "There isn't enough time...." or "It failed last time." Every suggestion is dismissed with "Yes, but that suggestion is no good." It doesn't take long for the "yes, buter" to render useless all of your ideas. Unable to come up with any more suggestions, you feel helpless. Without realizing it you lost control. You inadvertently took responsibility for solving the problem, while the disputant acts righteous in being burdened with this unsolvable conflict. Avoid this trap. Bite your tongue and *do not make suggestions.*

How To Elicit A Suggestion

You *elicit a suggestion by asking for one.* Turn to one of the disputants and ask, "What do you suggest?" Or "What do you suggest for resolving this?" Or "What do you suggest for solving this problem?" There are generally four kinds of responses a disputant can give: a denial, a reversal, an extreme, or a suggestion.

Denial

Often the disputant will answer your request for a suggestion with, "I don't know." Don't accept this. There are a number of reasons why a disputant might deny having any suggestion. Perhaps the disputant is embarrassed. The disputant might resist offering a suggestion for fear it will appear silly. Sometimes the disputant doesn't believe that you are sincerely interested in his or her suggestion. Often, disputants want you to coax them out.

Rule of Thumb: Don't accept a denial.

Ignore the "I don't know" and restate your request for a suggestion, a bit more firmly. The disputant may say, "I don't know" again. Alternatively, the disputant may answer, "What's the use?" Or "It's no use." Or "Why bother? He won't listen anyway." Ignore these various refusals to make a suggestion. Instead, persist in requesting one.

Persisting in your request for a suggestion puts pressure on the disputant to make one. Make sure you repeat your request at least three times. Use silence to increase the pressure for a suggestion. When the disputant doesn't give a suggestion ask, "What do *you* suggest?" firmly, then remain silent so that you communicate, "I expect you to solve this." Most disputants will offer some idea for resolution on the second or third request. This is particularly true when you are in a position of authority, such as being the disputant's supervisor, teacher, or parent for example.

Reversal

Sometimes disputants will attempt to reverse the process by responding with questions instead of a suggestion. "I don't know what to do. What would *you* do?" Resist the temptation to answer. Remember that when you start making suggestions you jump into King Solomon's shoes. Ignore the disputant's the request for a suggestion. Instead, restate your request for a suggestion more firmly.

Extreme

Another possibility is that the disputant offers an extreme or unworkable suggestion. The disputant might suggest, for example, that the adversary comply with everything he or she wants. Other times the disputant will request that you as the mediator take some kind of radical action such as "Fire him!" Or "Get that bum out of here." Or "Dock her pay." Or the disputant might suggest that he or she be given an unreasonable privilege.

The extreme suggestion is generally an attempt to divert the process, or a test to see whether you will respond with irritation. Don't go for the bait. When the disputant makes an extreme suggestion, just accept it at face value. This may be difficult to do. Just accept the suggestion without commenting on its reasonableness. If you say the suggestion is unreasonable you've stepped into the trap. The disputant will come back with something like, "I knew it. I knew you wouldn't listen to what I want."

EXAMPLE:

Mediator:	What do you suggest?
Ronnie:	Can his butt. I can do without him around here.
Poor:	What is a *reasonable* suggestion?
Ronnie:	Reasonable? You're not going to listen to me. Why bother?

Instead of commenting, take the ridiculous suggestion to the other disputant, who will not accept it.   In other words, avoid the trap by letting the disputant's adversary reject the suggestion as unworkable.

EXAMPLE:

Mediator:	What do you suggest?
Shelly:	I suggest that she pay me the entire $1000.
Mediator:	[To Ginger] Shelly suggests that you pay her the $1000. What do you think of that?
Ginger:	Well, that's just not reasonable.
Mediator:	What do *you* suggest, Ginger?
Ginger:	I suggest that deductions be made for the parts that haven't been completed.

An alternative and more effective approach is to accept the suggestion and use the information gathering techniques described in the last chapter to explore and clarify the suggestion. Disputants who are deliberately unreasonable tend to disavow the suggestion as your probing and checking out exposes its unreasonableness.   Sometimes a disputant's suggestion is sincere and the person doesn't understand how it might be seen as unreasonable by the other disputant or by you. Perhaps he or she hasn't thought it through, for example. Clarifying the suggestion often helps the disputant see it from his or her adversary's view.   Finally, there are time when what seems like an unreasonable suggestion is, in fact, a very good idea. Here if you reject the suggestion, you will probably alienate the disputant and hinder your ability to help the disputant find agreement.

EXAMPLE:

Mediator:	What do you suggest?
Ronnie:	Can his butt. I can do without him around here.
Better:	Do you mean your suggestion is that he be let go.
Ronnie:	You asked me. That's what I think.
Better:	[To Will] Ronnie thinks you should be let go. What do you think of that?
Will:	Well, that's unreasonable.
Better:	What do *you* suggest?
Will:	I suggest that Ronnie should be a little more negotiable and less pig-headed.
Better:	Negotiable?
Will:	He can be up front about what he wants.
Medaitor:	Up front? What do you want him to do?

No Suggestion

If you've made a number of firm requests for a suggestion and the disputant doesn't come up with any, turn to the other disputant and ask, "What do *you* suggest for solving this?" Be firm in communicating, "I expect you to solve this." When you communicate that you are serious, a suggestion will usually come.

Remember, each disputant has a hidden motive to appear to be the reasonable party in the conflict while the other disputant is the unreasonable person. When a disputant continues withholding suggestions, he or she starts looking like the unreasonable person! When you stand firm, repeating your request for a suggestion, one way for a disputant to look reasonable is to give a suggestion, preferably a reasonable suggestion.

When, after several requests, the first disputant has not offered any suggestion, then the second disputant can look very cooperative by merely giving a suggestion, thereby casting the other as uncooperative. On the other hand, if the second disputant fails to offer any idea for a resolution plan when you ask for one, continue to persist in asking. As stated before, mediation will not work in every situation. But don't give up prematurely. You lose little by keeping the pressure on for a suggestion.

Vague Suggestion

Sometime a disputant will offer an idea that you don't understand or that is so vague that you don't know what it is that he or she wants the other person to do.

> Mediator: What do you suggest for solving this?
> Disputant: Tell him to get off my back.

This may be something of an attack, but it is a kernel of a suggestion. However, it is not clear what the disputant is requesting. What does it mean to get off one's back? Use the information-gathering techniques to pull out a suggestion of what the disputant wants the adversary to do—on the doing level.

EXAMPLE:

> Disputant: I want him off my back!
> Mediator: Do you mean you want him to stop making evaluative comments on your performance?

EXAMPLE:

> Disputant: I want him off my back!
> Mediator: What do you want him to *do?*

EXAMPLE:

> Disputant: I want him off my back!
> Mediator: Off your back?
> Disputant: I want him to keep his lip buttoned.
> Mediator: Lip buttoned?
> Disputant: Tell him to stop putting me down in staff meetings.

Mediator: Do you mean you want him to refrain from commenting on your performance in staff meetings?

Disputant: Yeah. He can just shut up about me and focus on the project—or I'm out of here.

Mediator: Focus on the project?

Disputant: We're in the staff meeting to talk about the project, not about me. I want him to stick to the issue and get off my back.

Mediator: Do you mean that in staff meetings you want him to talk about issues pertaining to the project and refrain from commenting on your performance?

Disputant: Yeah! If he could do just that one thing, things would be a lot different around here.

Mediator: [Turning to the other disputant] James suggests in staff meetings that you focus your comments on issues pertaining to the project and not make comments about his performance. What do you think of that?

Often you'll get a well meaning suggestion but it is still unclear exactly what the disputant is asking that the adversary do. Even though it might seem redundant or tedious, it is important that you nail down the suggestion to a request for a specific change in behavior.

EXAMPLE:

Mediator: What do you suggest?

Disputant: He can be more friendly.

Mediator: More friendly? What do you want him to do?

Disputant: He can acknowledge me—you know, when he comes in, like he does the other people.

Mediator: What do you want him to do?

Disputant: I want him to say "Good morning" when he
comes in in the morning—like I was a
human being.

Often, the disputant hasn't thought past the vague demand. By drawing him or her out the mediator helps the disputant to formulate what change he or she wants.

PRESS FOR SPECIFIC CHANGE

Always work at the doing level with your objective being a specific behavior change in which each person knows what he or she is going to do. Getting the disputants to be specific in their requests for change makes for accountability. When the disputants agree to changes on the doing level, it is easy to see whether each person has carried out the plan. A person agreeing to be more friendly may be sincere, but his or her idea of more friendly may be different from what the adversary wants. It is hard to determine whether the person has been more friendly, and it if hard to know what is "more." On the other hand, if a person agrees to say "Good morning" when coming into the office, the disputant knows what he or she is expected to do, and other people can tell if it happened.

CHECK OUT THE SUGGESTION

When the suggestion has been nailed down to a specific behavior change, on the doing level, then check out the suggestion with the adversary. Turn to the adversary and repeat the suggestion, "Betty suggests that you..." and then ask, "What do you think of that?" Repeat the suggestion, even though the adversary heard it. In repeating the suggestion you exercise control. You are telling disputants when to talk, who will talk, and when to respond. Also, repeating the suggestion creates a certain degree of detachment. The second disputant can respond to you instead of the adversary.

The second disputant either refuses the suggestion or accepts and agrees to do it, in which case you are now well on the way to getting an agreement to a plan. When the disputant refuses the suggestion, immediately ask that person, "Okay, what do *you* suggest?" Disputants learn very quickly that if they refuse the other person's suggestion, the pressure will be on them to come up with a suggestion. If one fails to come up with a suggestion after rejecting the other person's suggestion, he or she looks like the unreasonable person.

EXAMPLE:

Tom: I suggest that Bill stops commenting on my spelling.

Mediator: [To Bill] Tom suggests that you not comment on his spelling. What do you think of that?

Bill: Well, I am going to comment on his spelling if he makes errors.

Mediator: What do you suggest, Bill?

Bill: He should proof read drafts first and not give me a mess.

Mediator: Do you mean that you suggest that Tom proofread drafts before giving them to you for review?

Bill: Yeah, only makes sense, right?

Mediator: [To Tom] Bill suggests that you proofread drafts before giving them to him. What do you think of that?

Tom: Okay. I can do *that.* I can use the spellchecker. But I want Bill to *stop* picking my work apart. He could find something right once in a while.

Mediator: Do you mean you want him to find something right about the draft to comment on?

Tom Well, that would be a good start.

Mediator: [To Bill] Tom says he'll run the spellchecker before giving you drafts for review, and he requests that you look for what is right about the draft to comment on. What do you think of that?

Essentially, you continue this process of eliciting a suggestion, clarifying that suggestion with interviewing techniques to get it down to the doing level, and then taking the suggestion to the other disputant. If the other disputant rejects the suggestion or part of the suggestion, then you elicit from that person an alternative suggestion which you then take back to the first disputant. The process continues like this, back and forth, until a mutually agreeable plan of action that is formulated.

When there are more than two disputants, make sure to check out the suggestion with each and every disputant, even though it seems redundant and laborious. *Don't skip anyone,* and don't allow one disputant to be a spokesperson for all the others.

REMAIN NEUTRAL

It is vitally important that you remain neutral. When you comment on a disputant's suggestion or cooperativeness, he or she is likely to feel you're being judgmental or otherwise taking sides.

EXAMPLE:

Mediator: Look, Milly's being very reasonable. You
            need to give in, too, you know.

Ralph: What's the use? You're always taking Milly's
            side.

Don't fall into this trap. Hold back and let Milly herself say if she thinks Ralph is not compromising. Do not comment upon or criticize suggestions. If a disputant's suggestion is unreasonable or extreme, rely on the other disputant to object to the suggestion. After all, it is their agreement, not yours.

DO NOT MAKE SUGGESTIONS

Don't offer suggestions—elicit them from the disputants. Your role is to help the disputants reach a mutually agreeable resolution. When you make suggestions you become responsible for the suggestion's success. If the plan fails, you are responsible to some degree. It is difficult to withhold your ideas, which may in fact, be very good. But they are your ideas, not the disputants. The objective is to facilitate the disputants resolving their disagreement at the same time that you teach them how to resolve future disputes. When you give suggestions you take away this opportunity from the disputants, at least to some degree. So, as difficult as it is to do, withhold offering your ideas, and focus on eliciting suggestions from the disputants.

ACCEPT SMALL CHANGES

Continue in the back and forth mediation process until the disputants agree on some specific change. Disputants may agree to act on only a portion of what seems to you like a larger problem, for example. Accept what you can get them to agree to, even if it seems one-sided, with one person giving in more and the other giving in less. The key is that the plan is agreed on by all the disputants.

Sometimes if a plan is too ambitious it will fail or work only in part. This is progress, nonetheless, because down the line you have an opportunity to refine the plan and make it a little more balanced.

REVIEW AND SUM UP THE PLAN

Use the review and sum up technique to determine when you've reached a mutually agreeable plan—only now follow the review with the question, "Is that agreed?" A "No" reply signals that you must continue to mediate. In that case ask, "Then what do you suggest?"

EXAMPLE:

Mediator: [Looking at Tom] Tom, you will make sure that the final copy of the monthly report is typed. Is that agreed?

Tom: No, not if I have to put up with Bill constant complaining about my spelling. A draft is a draft and it doesn't have to be perfect.

Mediator: Do you mean that to you it is okay to have errors in a draft because it is not the end product?

Tom: Exactly. But I'll accommodate Bill's sensi-
             tivities, and use the spelling checker, but he
             has to promise to focus on the report and
             refrain from his constant nit-picking about
             spelling—even if one mistake slips through!

Mediator: [Turning to Bill] Tom says he'll use the
             spelling checker on the drafts before giving
             them to Bill, if you agree to comment upon
             the subject of the report and not upon
             spelling errors, even if there are one or two.
             Is that agreed?

Bill: Yeah, no problem. That's got to be better
             than the messes he's been giving me.

When, on the other hand, the disputant answers, "Yes" to the
question, "Is that agreed?" turn to the next disputant and review what
you believe that person has ageed to do. When all disputants have
answered "Yes," that is the signal that you've reached a mutually agreeable plan.

EXAMPLE:

Mediator: [Looking at Tom] Tom, you will make sure
             that the final copy of the monthly report is
             typed without errors, if Bill makes no
             comments on your spelling when he reviews
             the draft. Is that agreed?

Tom   Sure, I can do that.

Mediator: [Turning to Bill] And Bill, you will read the
             drafts of the monthly report and comment
             on the content of the report only, not on
             Tom's spelling, if he agrees to make sure that
             the final copy is typed without errors. Is that
             agreed?

Bill: Yes, it makes a difference.

Mediator: Good! We've got a good plan here. Tom, you'll run the spelling checker on the drafts, and Bill, you will comment only on the context of the report, not the spelling.

ACKNOWLEDGE THE PLAN

Even when you think there are more layers to the dispute, if the disputants have agreed that each will do something differently, this is a beginning. This is where you have to start. People change in small steps. They need to learn that they can negotiate a plan.

Reward or reinforce disputants when they finally come up with a mutually agreeable plan. Say something like, "This sounds like a good plan. I think you've worked out something here." Acknowledge that the disputants have arrived at a plan.

PUT THE PLAN IN WRITING

A written plan adds importance to the agreement. Write the plan down so that everyone knows what has been agreed on and so that you and disputants can refer to it at a later time.

Furthermore, accountability is easier to achieve when the plan is written down. People tend to forget what they've agreed to. They can be quite innocent in this. We think that we agreed to one thing and when we actually agreed to something else, for example.

The plan doesn't have to be long, but it should be specific so that each disputant knows what he or she has agreed to do. *Make sure that every person involved in the mediation signs the agreement*—including yourself. For most people, the act of signing something holds a certain degree of psychological power. We sign binding contracts and checks. Signing the plan makes it official. The signature on the plan actually helps disputants make a commitment. They know that other people saw them signing the agreement which put pressure on them to live up to their agreement.

EXAMPLE:

> Mediator: In order to avoid confusion I'll write up a
>   memo confirming this agreement. After we
>   all sign it I'll make photocopies for each of
>   us.

Generally, the plan should stay among you and the disputants and not go into a personnel or academic file. Having such a document placed in one's file can be intimidating and put a damper on disputants' willingness to participate in mediation. Once something gets into an official file, it can be difficult to get it out. Taken out of context, the plan could be misunderstood—by a review committee or new supervisor, for example.

PLAN FOR FOLLOW UP

Whenever possible, schedule a follow-up and write it into the plan as part of the agreement.

EXAMPLE:

> Mediator: We'll meet in three days to discuss how this
>   plan is working.

The follow up session bolsters accountability. Disputants know that their following through on what they promised to do will be monitored. It gives a deadline and puts pressure on them to do what they've agreed on. Without the follow up it is easy for disputants to lose their resolve. Knowing that one is accountable is motivating—it moves people to act. For example, they can act to avoid the consequences of failing, or they can act to demonstrate that they are cooperative. When people know that their performance will be reviewed they tend to do better.

Equally important is the opportunity for feedback and shaping that a follow up meeting provides. Disputants are often unrealistic in their promises. They can mean well but overcommit themselves. They may have said they will do too much or promised too fast a change.

People change in small steps, not giant leaps. Other times the plan hasn't worked the way disputants had hoped it would. A follow up meeting gives an opportunity to make adjustments to the plan.

Important Point: People change in small steps.

When the plan is being carried out successfully, disputants may be motivated to carry the mediation one step farther. Successful change in small things encourages larger change. When this happens start the mediation process from the beginning. Conduct a new interview. You might start off with the question, "What do you suggest for making the plan better?"

Success sets the stage for more change. When disputants feel they have made some progress, even if it is on simple or trivial things, they see they are able to make an agreement which works, and this can lead to more substantial change.

If there has been some success and things are working, the follow up might be a time to probe into other areas. "Well, how are things going in general?" There may be other, latent conflicts the disputants are willing to discuss now that they've had some degree of success in solving their difficulties and relating to one another. But again, make sure to avoid leading questions. Whatever you do, don't start posing problems: "Well are you having problems in the staff meetings?" Don't invent problems.

Generally, control is less of a problem in the follow up meeting. Disputants have usually calmed down, and the encounter is not explosive. They know what to expect—they've seen how this operates, so that control is usually less of an issue.

When other people see that the disputants have been able to make some progress in their disagreements and difficulties in getting along with one another their success becomes a model. Remember, each problem you mediate successfully is actually a mini teaching session. You are teaching everybody in the setting, not just the particular disputants.

REWARD SUCCESS

Acknowledge disputants for the ways the plan has worked. Acknowledge the disputants' attempts even if the plan didn't work entirely. Focus on what *did* work. If you are in a situation in which you interact frequently with the disputants, you can help make the plan work. For example, look for occasions in daily routines when the disputants are carrying out the plan and then reward them. "Reward them" doesn't necessarily mean to go over and hand them some money or an M & M. There are all kinds of rewards. For example, if one person has agreed to say "Good morning" when he or she comes in, and then says it, you don't have to say something specifically and embarrass the person. Instead, you can nod in a knowing way, showing that you notice the effort.

Remember, it is hard for people to change. They need encouragement, they need rewards, and they need reminders. Your noticing ways that the disputants are succeeding is tremendously powerful in helping people carry out their agreements and in making behavior changes.

EXAMPLE:

> Coach: *Okay Alice, pick up at the summary.*
>
> Alice: [Looking at Sheila] "As you see it, Jeff left a
>   note asking you to put together a flyer,
>   which is not part of your job. So you put it
>   back on his desk and told him you were not
>   going to do it. Plus Jeff doesn't say "Hello"
>   to you when he comes in which makes you
>   feel ignored. [Looking at Jeff] And the way
>   you see it, Sheila said she would help you
>   with your flyer but then refused to help and
>   got angry when you left the mock-up on her
>   desk. You think that the way she acted is
>   unbusiness-like.

Coach:	*Now ask for a suggestion.*
Alice:	[To Sheila] What do you want Jeff to do?
Sheila:	Well, he could treat me with a little respect, for one thing.
Jeff:	Aw, come on, what is this, "Fix Jeff Week"?
Coach:	*What happened?*
Alice:	They're fighting again and I'm not getting anywhere.
Coach:	*Yes, and you sounded like you had taken Sheila's side when you asked what she wanted Jeff to do. Start again.*
Alice:	[To Sheila] What suggestions do you have for resolving this?
Sheila:	Well, I want Jeff to treat me with respect, instead of like a secretary.
Alice:	Treat you with respect? What do you want Jeff to do?
Sheila:	He could show me common courtesy. That's all, just a little courtesy.
Alice:	What do you want him to do?
Sheila:	Be polite. You know, like say, "Good morning," and ask, "How are you?" like any *normal* person.
Alice:	Do you mean that you want Jeff to greet you in a friendly way and inquire how you are?
Sheila:	It's just common courtesy. That's how he treats everyone else—with common courtesy. Why not me?
Alice:	[To Jeff] Sheila suggests that you treat her politely and show her common courtesy, like greeting her in a friendly way in the morning and inquiring how she is. What do you think of that?
Jeff:	I can't believe she cares about stuff like that! By her own admission, she hates me, so why....

Sheila:	See! See what he's like! He....
Alice:	[Raising her hand toward Sheila] Hold on, I'm talking to Jeff now.
Alice:	Do you mean that you will not agree to...
Jeff:	No. No! If it'll help, I'll go along with it.
Alice:	What will you do?
Coach:	*Good, Alice. Get him to be specific.*
Jeff:	Well, I'll be more courteous and make an effort to recognize Sheila. But I have a request, too.
Sheila:	Oh brother! I bet!
Alice:	[To Sheila] Hold on.
Jeff:	I want her to stop being such an aversary and be more of a team player.
Alice:	What do you want Sheila to do?
Coach:	*Good, get Jeff to explain on the doing level.*
Jeff:	We're here to help the public. But Sheila constantly quibbles over whether it's her job or my job. We should be working together to...
Sheila:	To do *your* recycling flyer, right Jeff?!
Alice:	Hold on, Sheila. [To Jeff] What do you suggest?
Jeff:	That we work together, instead of so much bickering.
Alice:	What do you suggest?
Jeff:	Shiela could be more helpful.
Alice:	Do you mean you want her help you with the recycling flyer?
Jeff:	Yeah, since she knows how to use those desktop programs and I don't.
Alice:	[To Sheila] Jeff suggests that you help him with the recycling flyer. What do you think of that?
Sheila:	You mean do it *for* him, since he can't do it!

	Why should I? It's his job, and he gets all the credit.
Jeff:	See, what's the use!
Alice:	Hold on, Jeff. [To Sheila] Gets all the credit?
Sheila:	He's the one who goes around introducing the program to the associations, and he's the one who goes to the banquet and accepts the merit award.
Alice:	*[To Coach] I'm stuck.*
Coach:	*How do you suppose Sheila would feel if she does the flyer for the program but Jeff gets an award at a banquet.*
Alice:	Like she's invisible and doesn't get credit for her contribution.
Coach:	*Okay, check that out with a feeling check.*
Alice:	Do you mean you feel invisible and unappreciated when you help Jeff and he gets the recognition.
Sheila:	Well, yeah. If I do the flyer why shouldn't I go to the banquet, too?
Alice:	*[To Coach] What do I do with that? Is it a suggestion?*
Coach:	*Can she go to the banquet?*
Alice:	There's nothing in the regulations that would prohibit it.
Coach:	*Then check it with a specific check.*
Alice:	Do you mean you will help Jeff with the flier if you can go to the awards banquet?
Sheila:	You mean *do* the flyer *for* Jeff. If he wants me to be a team player, then I ought to be able to go to the team celebration. Yeah, that's my suggestion.
Alice:	[To Jeff] Sheila suggests that she should be invited to the awards banquet, and if she is she will moch-up the flyer for you. What do you think of that?

Jeff: Hey, if she'll help me out on that flyer she
               can come to the banquet. Hell, she can sit
               at the head table.

Sheila: Don't get sarcastic.

Jeff: Who's sarcastic?

Alice: Hold on. Let me summarize. [To Sheila]
               You will be a team player on this project by
               helping Jeff moch-up the flyer for Jeff.
               [Turning to Jeff] You agree to be more
               courteous by recognizing Sheila, such as by
               saying, "Good morning," and making polite
               inquiries like, "How are you?" and so forth.
               And you will invite Sheila to the recycling
               program awards banquet. [To Sheila] Is
               that agreed?

Sheila: Yeah, it'll help—if he keeps his word!

Alice: Good! [To Jeff] Is that agreed?

Jeff: Yeah.

Alice: You've come up with a good plan. I think it
               will improve things. I'm going to summa-
               rize the plan in a memo, which I'll get to
               you later this afternoon.

Coach: *Remember to plan for a follow up.*

Alice: Okay, I want to meet with both of you again
               in a week to see how things are going. We'll
               meet at 2:00 in my office. Let's break now
               and get back to those busy phones.

The mediation has not addressed every one of Sheila and Jeff's concerns or obviated all of their resentments with one another. That's unrealistic. But the mediation has the potential for creating cooperation between Jeff and Sheila. If the results are good, they can build on this beginning.

EXAMPLE:

Coach:	*Okay, Dad, pick up at the summary.*
Father:	[To Mickey] You were waiting for the coach to call about practice, and you asked Sally to stay off the phone. But Sally got on the phone, and as a result you missed the call and the practice. [Turning to Sally] Because it was important to Mickey, you stayed off the phone for two hours. But he did not reciprocate, and instead he hung up on your important call. [Turning to Mickey] What do you suggest?
Mickey:	She could stay off the phone when I'm waiting for a call.
Coach:	*Accept that as a suggestion and take it to Sally.*
Father:	[To Sally] He suggests that you stay off the phone when he's expecting a call. What do you think of that?
Sally:	That doesn't work! Then he owns the phone while we wait, and I can't use the phone. No way!
Coach:	*Okay, she's rejected Mickey's suggest. Put pressure on her to come up with a suggestion by asking her for one.*
Father:	What do *you* suggest?
Sally:	Why can't he call the people he wants to talk to instead of waiting around for them to call him?
Coach:	*Take that suggestion to Mickey.*
Father:	[To Mickey] She suggests that you call people like the coach and your friends.
Mickey:	How can I call anyone when she is on the phone for hours?
Father:	Well, you could...

Coach:	*Watch out, you're falling into the trap of answering questions. Ask him again for a suggestion.*
Father:	What do you suggest?
Mickey:	Well, she could get off the phone once in a while.
Father:	Do you mean that you suggest she get off the phone periodically so that you can use it?
Coach:	*Good use of a check-out to clarify his suggestion.*
Mickey:	Right.
Father:	How often would she get off? What are you suggesting?
Mickey:	She could talk for a while and then be off the phone so I could use it for a while. Like she could talk for a half hour and then be off for a half hour.
Father:	[To Sally] He suggests that after you talk for a half hour you get off the phone for a half hour so that he can use it. What do you think of that?
Sally:	Well, I suppose...but who's going to keep track?
Father:	What do you suggest?
Sally:	We'd have to have a clock next to the phone. Look, I'll go along with this, but I want Mickey to be more considerate.
Father:	Considerate?
Coach:	*Good use of a repeat to clarify.*
Sally:	Yeah, I'm not going to put up with him yelling at me when I'm on the phone or hanging up on my calls.
Father:	What do you suggest? What do you want him to do?

Coach:	*Good, focus on the doing level.*
Sally:	He can stay out of the room.
Father:	Your sister suggests that you stay out of the room when she's on the phone. What do you think of that?
Mickey:	Well, I don't want to be in the room with her. But what if she goes over her time?
Sally:	He can write me a note.
Father:	She suggests that you remind her with a note.
Mickey:	Well, I'll try.
Coach:	*"Trying" is not good enough. Press him to accept or reject the suggestion.*
Father:	Do you mean that you agree to give her a reminder note if she goes over her time?
Coach:	*Good use of a check-out.*
Mickey:	Yeah. But how soon is she going to get off?"
Father:	Mickey says he'll give you a reminder note and wonders how soon you'll hang up.
Sally:	I'll hang up within five minutes. But I want him to recognize that I have important calls, too.
Father:	Recognize that your calls are important? What do you want him to do?
Coach:	*Good. You didn't accept the vague "recognize" but used a probe to press her to be specifc in her suggestion.*
Sally:	Well, he could begin by just saying that he recognizes that I have important calls.
Father:	[To Mickey] Sally said that she will hang up within five minutes of getting a reminder note, and she wants you to say that you recognize that she has important calls. What do you think?
Mickey:	This is stupid. Oh, okay, 'course she has important calls.

Father: [To Sally] What do you think?

Sally: He's not very convincing. Oh, okay, I'll accept it.

Coach: I think you've got an agreement here. Review and find out.

Father: [To Sally] You agree that you'll talk on the phone for only a half hour and then stay off for a half hour so that your brother can use it. If you forget, you'll get off within five minutes of Mickey giving you a note. [To Mickey] You agree to stay out of the room when she is on the phone, and if she goes over the half hour, you'll reminder her with a note. You also recognize that Sally has important calls, like you do.

Father: [To Mickey] Is that agreed?

Mickey: Yeah.

Father: [To Sally] Is that agreed?

Sally: Yeah.

Coach: Acknowledge the agreement and set a follow up.

Father: Well, I think we've got a good plan here. I'm going to write it down on this pad and we can all sign it like a contract. Then we each know what we agreed to do. And I want us to meet here again in three days, on Wednesday, to see how this goes.

By persisting and using the techniques effectively both Alice, the administrator, and the father were able to mediate agreements between the disputants. Of course, mediation won't always succeed. In the next chapter we'll examine what to do when mediation fails.

CHAPTER 6

WHEN MEDIATION FAILS

 $\mathcal{N}$ ot all attempts to mediate will be successful. Sometimes you will just not be able to get an agreement no matter how hard you try. When that happens you'll have to revert to one of the other options.

In certain circumstances, you might terminate someone or move one person to another area or department in order to keep the disputants apart. You might refer one or both to a specialist for assistance. More likely, you'll probably decide to do nothing, since there is only so much that you can do. When you are the person in authority, you might issue a directive. Issuing a directive under these conditions is generally the most likely alternative. But you must make sure you don't jump the gun. After several failed attempts to get the disputants to agree on a plan, you may have to take on the role of King Solomon and decide on a solution yourself.

In some cases, when you do give a directive and thereby become King Solomon, you must be very wise and very observant because it is your responsibility to figure out how to resolve or lessen this dispute. The key is to issue a directive that will *cause a change.*

REMOVE THE CONFLICT TRIGGER

Often there are certain kinds of situations that trigger conflict. People go along in relative peace until somebody does or says something that ignites the conflict. Identifying the conflict trigger can take a great deal of observation on your part. Sometimes it will come out in the interview. You might ask directly, "What triggers this?" If you have identified the conflict trigger, you can issue a directive that removes it.

Sally felt that Beth's requests for secretarial service were condescending and after several resolution attempts failed, the manager issued a directive that all requests for Sally's services would go through him. After that Beth did not ask Sally directly for the secretarial services, instead she placed the request with the manager who instructed Sally in carrying out secretarial services. By doing this the conflict trigger was removed. By stopping Sally and Beth from interacting directly the conflict trigger was eliminated.

CONTROL THE CONFLICT BEHAVIORS

Another option is to put limits or parameters on the conflict behaviors. For example, Harriet and Randy, two floor supervisors, were constantly bickering in front of subordinates over minute interpretations of departmental procedures. The manager felt that this confused employees and undermined Harriet's and Randy's authority. The conflict was controlled by imposing limitation on where and when they could argue. If they started bickering they were required to leave the floor and discuss the disputed issue in a closed office. They still argued but in a controlled way, one that did not hurt other people's productivity.

Another approach is to issue a directive of when and how these people agree to fight. An injunction against two-on-one fights is an example. Here people are told that only one-on-one arguing is permissable, and that two people beating down one person is not acceptable. Personal attacks can be prohibited. Of course, few people admit to having made personal attacks. The problem is that people who make such attacks usually insist they are not making a personal attack—don't realize they are doing it, or they don't know what a personal attack is. Personal attacks are hard to control with a directive. A personal attack is something like, "If you were doing a better job at home you wouldn't be such a bear at work!"

ALTER THE CONSEQUENCES OF THE CONFLICT

Another approach is to focus on the consequences of arguing. Identifying the outcome of the conflict requires a lot of observation on your part. Does one person always win? Perhaps one disputant gets sympathy from other people? "Gee Ralph, that was awful. Let's go to lunch and talk about it." The consequence for Ralph is sympathy: going out to lunch and attention. Sometimes a person gets praised: "Boy, I've got to hand it to you. You sure came across when the chips were down." Once again the disputant is rewarded for arguing.

Sometimes, without realizing it, you reward the fighting behavior. Obviously, you don't want to do this. That's why it is important for you to observe objectively what happens *after* the conflict. Notice who gets rewarded, where there is praise, where there is attention. Notice the results of the conflict. Often other people in the setting maintain fighting behavior between people by the way they respond to the fights. Sometimes you can set up a situation in which everybody is rewarded for less conflict. For example, you might let people go home an hour early on Fridays after a conflict-free week, for example. Under such a plan everyone has an incentive to stop conflicts which curtails sympathizing with disputants

WHEN TO INITIATE CONFLICT RESOLUTION

When you perceive tension among employees you are within the realm of your authority as a boss to say, "I'd like the two of you to sit down and talk." Your job as a supervisor is to deal with work-related situations; and if you feel there is a situation that is adversely affecting workplace performance, it is within your realm of responsibility to deal with it. When the conflict is not out in the open is a proble. If you approach the disputants about it, they may well act as though they don't know what you're talking about. And therein is the dilemma. You're in something of a "Catch 22" situation.

By the same token, however, when you deal with other disputes by using the conflict resolution process, those involved in underground conflicts will hear about it. When you conduct mediation you are not only helping to resolve the particular conflict at hand, but you are also simultaneously teaching your staff how to solve future disagreements. By consistently handling conflicts directly and matter-of-factly, as everyday occurrences in the workplace, you create a conducive atmosphere for the open handling of disagreements. You communicate that festering and stewing on hassles is not acceptable and that you expect people to negotiate resolutions to their disagreements.

It would be nice if we could wave a magic wand and always get an answer for everything. But all we can do realistically is to create an ambience in the workplace that encourages the open discussion of disagreements.

WHEN DISPUTANTS TRULY DISLIKE ONE ANOTHER

It is not realistic to expect that all people will like each other. But a person's annoyance for another does not make it acceptable for that person to sabotage the other. People are expected to be team players regardless of their personal feelings. On work teams and sports teams alike each person has a position to play and people are expected to "set each other up"—to score and to throw the ball to the runner—regardless of how much they like or don't like the other person. Liking the person is irrelevant. You don't have to like someone to throw them the ball so that the team can win.

It is this concept of team play that supervisors need to communicate to their staffs, and teachers to their students. If you're confronted with a disputant who says, "Look, I just don't like so-and-so and no matter haw many talks we have, I'm not going to like her," your response should be, "Fine. Nobody is asking you to like her. However, regardless of your feelings you must work cooperatively with her and throw her the ball. That's your job. If you can't do that, then there's a problem, and the problem is that you are not doing your job, which will lead to a negative evaluation and a black mark in your file." When you project this kind of standard, you've changed things. The disputant is allowed to like or dislike whom ever he or she pleases, but it does not become the basis for undermining a co-worker.

HOW TO HANDLE RETICENT DISPUTANTS

Some disputants will resist telling you about their conflict. Often, they will stonewall you with silence and brief answers. Interviewing such disputants is difficult and nerve-wracking. But if you persist and use the techniques well, you can pull the information out of most disputants.

EXAMPLE:

Mediator:	Pam, what is the situation as you see it?
Pam:	It's just a lost cause.
Mediator:	Lost cause?" (repeat)

Pam:	I don't want to talk about it. I don't...
Ralph:	[Interrupting] Well, I don't want to....
Pam:	See! He interrupts me all the time!
Mediator:	[Waving a hand toward Ralph] Hold on. [Tapping his chest with his hand and looking at Pam] Talk to me. (redirecting attention to mediator)
Pam:	Aw, I don't know, it's just not worth it. I just don't care.
Mediator:	What's not worth it? (probe)
Pam:	This whole thing!
Mediator:	Whole thing? (repeat)
Pam:	He just criticizes me. He degrades every thing.
Mediator:	What does he say? (probe)
Pam:	He saids, "I'm incapable" and just that kind of thing.
Mediator:	What kind of thing? (probe)
Pam:	That kind of comment.
Mediator:	What kind of comment? (probe)
Pam:	Condescending!
Mediator:	Uh-huh.... (silence)
Ralph:	I did not.
Pam:	See! [Turning toward Ralph] You just be quiet for once!
Mediator:	[Holding up his hands, with palms facing out toward each disputant] Hold on!. Now I want to know how each of you sees the problem. I'm going to talk with you one at a time. I've heard Ralph's side, and now I want to hear Pam's side." (using hand gestures to apply force and repeating ground rules to regain control) [Withdrawing hands, and turning toward Pam] What's happening, Pam? (probe)

Pam: I just don't want to talk about it. It's just too tiring.

Mediator: Just tell me how *you* see it.

Pam: I'm just so frustrated.

Mediator: Frustrated? (repeat)

Pam: Yeah, in staff meetings he just dominates.

Mediator: Dominates? (repeat)

Pam: I try to say something, but he just keeps talking, or he puts me down, so I give up.

Mediator: Let's see if I understand this. As *you* see it, what happens is that when you're in a staff meeting, the way that Ralph acts and speaks makes it difficult for you to get your comments in. Is there anything else? (review)

Pam: There's more to it than that. It's really hard to talk. I want Ralph to listen and not always to interrupt so that I can have my say once in a while. We're supposed to be co-leaders. [turning to Ralph] I don't think I can work with you.

Mediator: [Leaning forward to cut off Pam's view of Ralph] Talk to me, Pam. (redirecting at tention to mediator)

Ralph: Wait a minute here.

Mediator: [Ignoring Ralph and looking at Pam] The way you see it, if the two of you are going to work together on this project as co-leaders, you feel that you must have your say. But when Ralph interrupts, you can't say your point. Is there anything else? (review)

Pam: That's not exactly how I feel.

Mediator: How do you feel? (probe)

Pam: I'm annoyed.

Mediator:	What's annoying? (probe)
Pam:	He's not my boss. In staff meetings he makes comments about my performance, and I just think it's out of line.
Mediator:	Do you mean that in front of others in staff meetings he makes evaluative comments about your performance as if he were your boss? (check-out)
Pam:	Yes. Don't you think it's wrong of him?
Mediator:	[Ignoring Pam's question] As you see it, the two of you have to work together as co-leaders with equal authority, but you think Ralph makes it unequal by making evaluative comments about your performance to co-workers and this concerns you because you don't see how you can work together under these conditions. Is there anything else? (review)
Pam:	No, that's it.

You can see in this example that it takes paying very close attention to what the disputant has said and then skillfully using probes, repeats, check-outs and summaries to draw the person out. Often a person will protest that he or she knows little and has little to say. Yet, skillful use of the information-gathering techniques can reveal that the person knows much more than indicated.

EXAMPLE:

Interviewer:	What do you know about astrology?
Subject:	I don't know anything about that ridiculous stuff.
Interviewer:	Ridiculous?
Subject:	Yeah, it's a lot of metaphysical mumbo-jumbo.
Interviewer:	Metaphysical mumbo-jumbo?

Subject:	This California cosmic stuff about stars and moons influencing your life.
Interviewer:	How does it work?
Subject:	They make a chart of stars based on your birth date and think that should tell you how to live. Like I said, I really don't know anything about it.

When the Subject said "ridiculous stuff" it became apparent that the Subject knew something in order to draw the conclusion that astrology is ridiculous. By focusing in on these kinds of comments and using the interviewing techniques well, the Interviewer was able to draw out the Subject's knowledge of astrology.

WHEN YOU CAN'T GET TO THE DOING LEVEL

Sometimes you'll have made every attempt to review and sum up the core issue, but disputants remain vague in their complaints no matter how well you use the techniques. If you reach a stalemate and can't nail down the disagreement to the doing level, it may appropriate to try to pull together a mutually agreeable plan even though what each disputant agrees to do is not as specific as you'd like it to be. It is important not to do this prematurely.

CHAPTER 7

WHEN YOU ARE A DISPUTANT

*W*hen you are involved in a conflict you are, by definition, a disputant. As a disputant you can't mediate, because mediation presupposes an objective, disinterested party. Nonetheless, you can employ the same approach and techniques to *negotiate* a resolution. If you want to be successful your objective should be to resolve the conflict in a win-win manner. This means you must assert your needs and priorities without being unreasonable or overbearing, while you're also being attentive that your adversary wins too. I highly recommend that you attend a workshop or read a book on being assertive.

There are a lot of approaches to assertiveness. Some encourage using one-liners, sometimes called the "broken record technique." Here, you repeat—over and over like a broken record—a statement or "one-liner," such as "I'm not interested" to your adversary's demands. This sort of approach is good for unsolicited sales pitches on the telephone, for example. You can get the pest off your  back without getting sucked into an unwanted purchase. But when dealing with a co-worker or friend, these techniques have great limitations. You may assert your position, but such an approach doesn't resolve the conflict or bring about change. Furthermore, your adversary is likely to experience you as a steamroller rolling right over his or her concerns.

INTERVIEW YOUR ADVERSARY

You can use the conflict interview techniques described here—but it takes a great deal of presence of mind. When your adversary says, "You dirty rotten so-and-so, you..., instead of reacting to the attack or counterattacking, you can ask, "What did I do?" Then employ the other interview techniques in order to get a good understanding of the problem as your adversary sees it.

When you are in a supervisory position or some other authority role and someone attacks or criticizes you, you can be thrust into a double-bind, damned-if-you-do-damned-if-you-don't situation. If you absorb the attack, you can appear weak and lose power in the eyes of others; if, on the other hand, you attack back, you lose credibility. Let's face it, it is awfully hard to resist snapping back with some sort of a dig, especially when the attack on you is unwarranted.

If, on the other hand, you keep your cool and move into a disputant interview, you look professional and can actually enhance your credibility and power. This is not easy, but with practice and presence of mind you can do it.

When attacked or criticized, say nothing. Resist defending, justifying, or attacking back. Instead, proceed with a dispute interview and continue to ask questions until your adversary has nothing more to say. Then review and sum up.

EXAMPLE:

Adversary:	You are just a bum!
You:	Bum?
Adversary:	Yeah, you are an idiot. I just can't believe how stupid you can be!
You:	What did I do?
Adversary:	You....

Continue with the dispute interview, being careful never to state your opinion or attack back. You will hear things that you will hate hearing. Don't respond! Instead, keep *yourself* under control. Ask questions and draw that your adversary. Make sure that you press him or her to describe the problem completely. If you can resist the temptation to defend and attack, you'll notice a curious thing. The adversary will very quickly calm down and speak much more reasonably, with fewer attacks and exaggerations. You see, you are in control and you look calm and professional; in contrast, the ranting adversary, hurling insults and exaggerations, looks silly—if not down right inappropriate. The next step is for you to review and sum up.

EXAMPLE:

You:	So, as you see it, you feel that I have been "playing favorites" by giving the good assignments to Joseph here, while giving you the "grunt" jobs. Additionally, you think that my supervisory style is poor, and that I should either resign or get some professional training. Is there anything else?
Adversary:	Yeah, uh, look, you said in the staff meeting that we should be open about our feelings, didn't you? I am just trying to tell you that I need to have better assignments.
You:	Yes, I'm glad you brought this to my attention. I'll think over what you said, and we'll meet tomorrow at 2 p.m. to discuss your projects. [Looking at your watch] I have an appointment in a few minutes, so I will close this discussion now.

You have turned the tables. Furthermore, you have drawn out the festering venom. You know what the adversary is thinking and what is bother him or her. You have defused his or her anger. The adversary, on the other hand, had gotten virtually nothing from you and has not pushed you into "blowing your cool."

After leaving the situation you can call a confidant or go into your office and "freak out" behind closed doors, outside the view of your staff. Furthermore, you now have an opportunity to think over what the  adversary has said. Perhaps there is some truth to his or her complaint; perhaps he or she is right and you have, in fact, played favorites or been unreasonable in some way. You can come up with a plan for handling the problem and correcting your errors without losing face, so to speak.

The dispute interview techniques, when used correctly, are very powerful. The problem is that we often forget. Instead, we resort to a knee-jerk mode. We see the red flag and become like the bull, snorting and pawing in the dirt.

SHOW EMPATHY

When mediating, it is important to communicate that you understand the disputants' viewpoints—yet you must be careful to not appear to be taking sides by always projecting impartiality. When negotiating, by contrast, you are a disputant with your own opinion about the conflict, and that opinion is part of the dispute. In other words, you are biased and not objective. Your adversary, the other disputant or disputants with whom are you negotiating, assume that you are biased. This makes communicating that you understand, and showing empathy, vitally important. Understanding and empathy differ only in degree. When communicating understanding you demonstrate that you grasp how your adversary views the situation; when showing empathy, you demonstrate that you understand how he or she feels about it.

Seeing the situation as the other side sees it is essential because the conflict is not in the situation but in the *conflicting views* of the situation. If you are to negotiate a workable agreement you must get the conflict out in the clear and examine it. That is, you must uncover the differences in the ways that you and your adversary view the conflict.

Interview your adversary with the objective of finding out how he or she sees the situation and discovering his or her basic concern. Use a probe and ask, "What is the problem *as you see it?*" Or, "What is *your* basic concern?" Even if you are positive that you already understand your adversary's position, don't make assumptions. Ask instead, "What happened?" or "What did I say that sounded like that?", for example.

Unexpressed emotions or feelings that have been pushed underground can resurface in unexpected ways to cause an impasse. Angry and hurt feelings are a natural response to frustration. Elicit emotions and put yourself into your adverary's shoes. Remember that understanding something doesn't mean you agree with it; empathizing with another's dilemma doesn't mean that you feel the same way. You can help your adversary express feelings by asking, "How do you feel about this?" or "How did that affect you?"

Just asking for feelings is not enough, of course. Momentarily let go of yourself while you listen in order to see the situation as your adversary does. Put yourself into your adversary's shoes and try to imagine the dispute from his or her position. Then communicate this understanding. The check-out technique works well. You can ask, "Do you mean...?" or "Tell me if I understand what you are saying." Alternatively, you can restate with a summary: "As you see it, the problem is...." or "As I understand it, your concerns are...."

AVOID BLAME

Avoid blame when interviewing your adversary. Nothing shuts down negotiations faster than "the blame game." The minute you begin to affix blame, your adversary will become defensive and will counterattack or shut down altogether. Being nonjudgmental and getting specific information instead of jumping to conclusions is as important to negotiating as it is to mediating. Check-out frequently by asking, "Do you mean...?"

Just like in mediation, when the mediator must keep disputants under control, as negotiator you must exert control. Don't be surprised if your adversary becomes angry when explaining her or his side. Expect outbursts. Consider it an opportunity for your adversary to blow off steam. Don't react, don't defend; defuse instead. Reframe personal attacks as attacks on the problem. Doing this is a challenge, because keeping your wits about you and controlling yourself will be difficult when you hear you adversary's attacks.

GIVE INFORMATION

Negotiation and mediation differ most in respect from your giving information. When mediating you must be impartial, but when negotiating you are a party in the dispute. In order to be effective in mediating you must withhold your opinions and feelings about the situation; whereas when negotiating, success comes in part from a skillful presentation of your concerns.

DESCRIBE YOUR PICTURE OF THE CONFLICT

If you are going to negotiate an agreement that meets your concerns, you'd best know what your concerns are. This may seem to go without saying, except that we often find ourselves in a conflict without having thought through our concerns.

Describe the problem as you see it to your adversary while keeping in mind the guidelines we explored earlier, for example. Saying something like, "The problem is your constant childish demands for attention" will probably aggravate your adversary. Not only is such a problem statement vague—we don't know what the person is *doing*,—but it is loaded with judgmental and emotional labels and innuedoes. Instead, state "just the facts, Ma'am." Be specific instead and describe situations, behaviors, or outcomes. You can say, "You interrupted my phone call a few moments ago, and you've interrupted many phone calls in the past" instead of "your childish demands for attention".

Just as you should avoid blaming or attacking your adversary, you should avoid defending and justifying your concerns. Not only do your defenses tend to sound like attacks to your adversary, but repeating them tends to get each of you entrenched in your "positions." Instead, be concise. Stick to one concern; don't throw in every annoyance. Get to "just the facts, Ma'am." Don't ramble and repeat.

EXPRESS YOUR CONCERNS AND FEELINGS

It helps to separate the facts of the situation—as you see them—from your concerns and feelings about those facts. Two important points need to be empahsized here. First, even though we think that "facts are facts" and therefore reflect "reality," your adversary may well perceive the "facts" to be different or may see the same facts differently. Rather than trying to get consensus on the exact "facts" of the dispute, it works better to get an understanding of how you and your adversary each view it.

In assertiveness training you're usually encouraged to identify your needs and separate your feelings from events so that you can be proactive instead of reactive. That is, you can initiate action to get what you need instead of reacting to the moment and caving in or lashing out. These same insights and skills apply when stating your side during negotiations.

USE "I" STATEMENTS

As you might guess from the description, "I" statements are statements of your feelings or reactions that begin with "I." Returning to the phone interruption example, you could say, "You interrupted me when I was on the phone with an important account. When this happens, I get distracted in my sales pitch and lose credibility with the customer." First describe the facts of the event—what happened and who did or said what to whom—without judgmental or emotional embellishment. Follow with the "I" statement—the statement of your feelings or concerns about the event.

The "I" statement focuses on your feelings and your concerns only. Avoid blaming or speculating about your adversary's motives. A statement like, "I feel you are so rude and disrespectful that you're trying to undermine me" is not an "I" statement. Instead of expressing your feelings and what happens to you, it blames and accuses your adversary. Avoid this. Tell how the situation impacts you, not what you think your adversary did and why.

NEGOTIATE AN ACTION PLAN

It's tempting to move quickly to making suggestions to solve to the dispute. This is a mistake. You need a good understanding of how you and your adversary see the situation, because the key to negotiating a win-win agreement lies in understanding these conflicting perceptions.

When functioning both as negotiator and disputant, it's generally best if you begin by interviewing your disputant first. Re-read the guidelines and techniques described for mediation, and use them. Take as much time as necessary. Avoid jumping to conclusions by making frequent summaries of your understanding of your adversary's view: "The problem as you see it... (+ summary)" followed by "Is there anything else?" or "Is that how you see it?"

When you communicate understanding and empathy your adversary is more receptive to seeing your side. Additionally, you've demonstrated how to communicate understanding. So in most cases it is probably most effective to uncover your adversary's view before telling your side. There can be exceptions, of course, such as when someone is self-conscious about expressing feelings. Here you might share your side first.

Once again, negotiating and mediating are very similar. The major difference is that in negotiating you will be commenting on your adversary's suggestions and making suggestions of your own, which is to be avoided in mediating.

MAKE SUGGESTIONS

The first step is to get the process rolling by getting some suggestions out on the table. It's tempting to push your suggestions forward right away, but it's more effective to hold back and elicit suggestions from your adversary first. Elicit suggestions in the same way that the mediator does. After summarizing his or her view of the situation, ask your adversary, "What do you suggest?" or "What ideas do you have, June, for breaking through this?" or "What do you think we ought to do here, Bill?"

If you don't get a suggestion right away, persist. Your adversary may wonder about your sincerity in inviting his or her suggestions. Try different words—ones more inviting to your adversary. "What's your preference?" might be more effective with a disputant in eliciting a suggestion, for example. When you get a suggestion, flesh it out by asking for clarification—"What do you want me to do?" or "How would that help?"—and checking out your understanding—"Do you mean...?" Take your time. Summarize the suggestion with "You suggest...(+ summarized suggestion).... Is there anything else?"

When you offer suggestions follow the guidelines given for describing your concern. Be specific in what you want: who will do what. Be brief, describing one suggestion at a time. Avoid emotional words and accusations. Follow your suggestion with a request for comment. "What do you think of that?" or "How would this work for you?"

Negotiation is a back-and-forth process in which an agreement slowly emerges. So take your time. Use the mediation techniques to stay on course.

TIPS FOR MORE SUCCESSFUL NEGOTIATIONS

Avoid either/or and all-or-nothing thinking, which tends to turn negotiations into a tug-of-war in which one person gets more of his or her way. Generally, there are a variety of workable solutions to most conflicts. Think "both/and" and strive to find solutions that satisfy the needs of both you and your adversary. Evaluate suggestions in terms of possible joint gain.

Along these lines, look for areas of shared interest. Everyone negotiates something every day. Negotiation is our basic method of getting what we want from others. Negotiation as back-and-forth communication designed to reach an agreement when you and the other side have some interests that are shared and others that are opposed. Mediation is a similar back-and-forth communication facilitated by an impartial person.

Shared interests are concerns that you both have in common. Focusing on mutuality helps break down adversarial posturing. When you bring out areas of shared concern you and your adversary are more receptive to suggestions that serve both your interests. These areas of agreement can then be expanded on to address certain independent concerns. In some cases you and your adversary will have interlocking or complementary concerns. The child's nursery rhyme, *Jack Spratt* illustrates this. Jack Spratt could eat no fat and his wife could eat no lean. But together they licked the platter clean.

Look for ways to "give in" to your adversary. The more your adversary feels like he or she is getting satisfaction from the negotiation, the more open and agreeable that person is likely to be. Give in on the less important points, especially when one is of great importance to your adversary.

Build a bridge of agreement between you and your adversary. This includes negotiations that lead to agreements about where you disagree. Another approach is to break the problem into pieces, then agree on which sub-problem should be tackled and how. While these techniques don't lead to an immediate "solution" to the problem, they help negotiations. At the very least, they give you and your adversary an opportunity to agree on something. In the process you learn how to negotiate and get some sense of success. So, efforts spent in further defining the nature and scope of the dispute are worthwhile because they set the stage for agreement.

State what your adversary has to gain by meeting your needs. Instead of negativity, threats, and conflict, hold out the carrot. To do this skillfully you need first to understand how your adversary sees the situation and what your adversary wants to gain.

USE A MEDIATOR

It is certainly a challenge to negotiate a mutually satisfying agreement in a conflict situation when you are one of the disputants. Even the most skilled professional would have difficulty. Using a mediator can side-step this problem. The facilitator assumes the role of mediator and follows the approach described earlier. Of course, your adversary must feel confident in choice of facilitators. Deciding to use a mediator and determining who that person will be can be the goal of your self-directed negotiations. The mediator must be seen as neutral and must be strong enough to command your attention if the discussions should degenerate into bickering or a verbal clash. Mediators can be friends, co-workers, clergy, or professional counselors, for example.

DISPUTE PREVENTION

While conflict itself isn't bad, poorly handled disputes can cause stress and disruption. The best way to prevent disruptive conflict is to build a good working relationship with the disputant as well as others with whom you frequently interact. Disagreements arise frequently—especially over seemingly small things. These negotiation opportunities offer a chance to build a good "working" relationship and set a tone that encourages the clarification of disagreements and the seeking of creative solutions. It is also your opportunity to practice the various steps of mediation. For example, you can elicit a co-worker's concerns about a particular phase of a project you are working on together. You can practice using probes for getting facts, check-outs for clarifying, and summaries for communicating understanding.

Group situations like committee meetings and even office social occasions offer opportunities for you to step into the mediation role when, for example, committee members are discussing various views on a subject. For example, you can clarify the viewpoint of a member who is ambiguous ("George, do you mean...?"), or draw out ideas from someone who has been silent ("Shirley, what is your view of this situation?") Then summarize with "To review, George, your idea is + (suggestions). What do the rest of you think of that suggestion?" Or "Shirley, as you see it.... Is there anything else?"

In developing a good working relationship you don't strive to eliminate disagreement. Instead, you deal with the disagreement in the normal course of working together so that it doesn't grow into a dispute because you have developed trust and a give-and-take expectation.

Index

ABOUT THE ARTIST BEHIND THE ART

Phil Frank, creator of the exclusive *San Francisco Chronicle* comic strip *Farley,* has demonstrated, once again, in this work that he understands the art of communicating with humor. Frank's cartoons have been featured in local and national shows and numerous award-winning publications.

Phil Frank's cartooning talent is available in the MEGATOONS clip art collections in which signature illustrations are delivered on disks or CD ROM.

For information, contact Creative Media Services, PO Box 5955, Berkeley, CA 94705 or 800-358-2278.

BOOK COVER DESIGNER

BRIAN GROPPE

c/o

TOWERY PUBLISHING, INC.

1835 UNION AVENUE

SUITE 142

MEMPHIS, TN 38104

901 725 2400

FINDING A PATH WITH A HEART

How To Go From Burnout To Bliss

Dr. Beverly Potter

In today's workplace you must solve problems rather than just complete repetitive tasks, and lead yourself rather than wait to be told what to do. *Finding A Path With A Heart* shows how to become a self-leader—a pathfinder—finding a way to your bliss in your work.

When following a path with a heart you feel at one with what you are doing. Attention is highly focused and actions seem effortless, almost sponta- neous. You can achieve optimal performance, be more innovative and get your job done while experiencing many moments of bliss.

Finding A Path With A Heart is an engaging guide sprinkled with drawings, stories, exercises and quotes. You'll learn why you're more likely to experience bliss while at work than in leisure, how you can increase your potential for achieving it, and discover 12 self-leadership tools for finding your path to more bliss in work and play while performing at your peak.

Business/Careers

3 66 pp

Illustrations

Appendix

$14.95

ISBN 0-914171-74-7

"Cock-full of good ideas, interestingly put together...tremendously informative and helpful.."
— Mihaly Csikszentmihalyi
author of *Flow: The Psychology of Optimal Experience*

"Worth reading!!!"
—Marty Edelson
president, Boardroom, Inc.

"...practical, readable, imaginative, non-linear, creative and filled with doable ideas."
—John D. Krumboltz
professor, Stanford University

BEATING JOB BURNOUT
How To Transform Work Pressure
Into Productivity
Second Edition
Dr. Beverly Potter

Beating Job Burnout tells how to renew enthusiasm for work by developing personal power. This upbeat guide shows how to recognize job burnout and overcome it through a progression of positive changes, including setting goals, managing stress, building a strong social support system, modifying the job, developing needed skills, changing jobs, modifying powerless thinking and developing detached concern.

Beating Job Burnout provides information managers, counselors, and individuals can utilize to eliminate feelings of powerlessness on the job. Includes a revision of the "Burnout Potential Inventory." **Winner of the** *American Journal of Nursing* **"Books of the Year" Award.**

Career/Self-help
306 pp
Illustrations
Appendix
Questionnaires
$12.95
ISBN 0-914171-69-0

PREVENTING JOB BURNOUT
A Workbook
Second Edition
Dr. Beverly Potter

Preventing Job Burnout is a hands-on workbook which guides you step-by-step through the change process. Filled with checklists and worksheets, this power-packed workbooks allows individuals to progress at thair own pace. It is an excellent resource for groups and classes. Very practical.

"If it's possible to cure burnout with a book, this one could do it."
— Savvy Magazine

112 pp
Worksheets
Questionnaires
$9.95
ISBN 1-56052-357-3

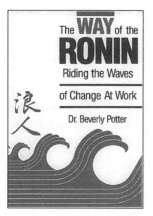

Career/Self-help

252 pp

Illustrations

Appendix

$9.95

0-914171-26-7

THE WAY OF THE RONIN
Riding The Waves Of Change At Work

Dr. Beverly Potter

The Way of the Ronin offers an inspiring strategy for handling change while performing excellently in today's workplace.

Ronin or "wave-men" were masterless samurai. To survive they became their own masters to live by their swords. When feudalism collapsed it was the ronin who led the way to industrialize Japan. *The Way of the Ronin* tells how to be excellent and self-mastering like a warrior and how to deal with "corporate feudalism"—a rigid system that resists change and that tries to squelch your spirit.

First published by The American Management Association, *The Way of the Ronin* draws upon the wisdom of philosophers, the findings of trend watchers, the latest research of management experts and the technology of behavior psychology to show how to:

- Thrive on change
- Tell excellence from perfectionism
- Turn enemies into allies
- Become a workplace warrior
- Manage self-starters
- Develop maverick career strategies

"Intelligent and inspiring book."
　　　　　　　　　　　　　　　　—ALA Booklist

"One of the best business books of the year."
　　　　　　　　　　　　　　　—Library Journal

"A mix of zen and behavior modification, case histories, thought-control exercises, and goal-setting tips."
　　　　　　　　　　　　　　　　　　—The Argus

TURNING AROUND
Keys To Motivation And Productivity
Beverly Potter, Ph.D.

Turning Around shows step-by-step how to assure top performance from yourself and all those on your team. It explains the most complex techniques in down-to-earth terms.

Turning Around explains behavior psychology and how to apply the techniques to daily supervision situations. It is a valuable reference to return to when faced with difficult management questions. *Turning Around* tells how to:

- Use behavior modification
- Conduct interviews
- Lead meetings
- Mediate conflicts
- Manage authority
- Manage yourself.

Turning Around focuses strictly on objectives and how to achieve them day-in and day-out. It makes your job easier and your career progress more satisfying.

"Best book on the topic."
       —Personnel Psychology

"Fresh insight in the area of motivation by kindness and compassion."
       —Special Libraries

Management/ Psychology
292 pp
Illustrations
Appendix
Index
$9.95
0-914171-16-X

LECTURES & SEMINARS BY DR. BEVERLY POTTER

Dr. Beverly Potter is a dynamic speaker and experienced seminar leader. Topics include:

✦ Finding a Path With a Heart
✦ Managing Yourself for Excellence
✦ Feeding the Brain for Peak Performance
✦ Beating Job Burnout
✦ Managing Work Stress
✦ High Performance Goal Setting
✦ From Conflict to Cooperation
✦ Secrets of Effective Interviewing
✦ Managing Authority

"Potter is infectious, gregarious, boisterous, intense and engaging."
–Toronto Sun

"The program was... certainly a highlight..."
–California State Bar Association

"...helpful and motiva-ting..."
–Stanford University Library

Programs can be tailored to your group's needs. For more information, call Dr. Beverly Potter at **510-540-6278.**

BEATING JOB BURNOUT
How To Increase Job Satisfaction

Dr. Beverly Potter

A lively and informative interview in which Dr. Potter describes the symptoms and causes of job burnout and what to do about it. Based on Dr. Potter's book *Beating Job Burnout.* Originally produced by *Psychology Today* Cassette Program.

$9.95
Audio cassette, 60 minutes
ISBN 0-914171-41-0

MAVERICK AS MASTER IN THE MARKETPLACE
The Way of the Office Warrior

Dr. Beverly Potter
Interview by Michael Toms

An inspiring interview with Dr. Beverly Potter by Michael Toms, host of New Dimensions Radio, featured on over 100 National Public Radio shows. *Maverick As Master in the Marketplace* provides insights to empower the independent minded to rise above corporate feudalism and get ahead while enjoying it more.

$9.95
Audio cassette, 60 minutes
ISBN 0-914171-42-9

Drug Testing at Work
Guide for Employers and Employees

Beverly Potter, Ph.D.
Sebastian Orfali, M.A.
$17.95, 252 pp.
0-914171-32-1

"A valuable reference."
    –Dr. David Smith

"Balanced . . . very good."
    –Dr. Alexander Shulgin

Drug Testing at Work is a comprehensive guide to drug testing in the workplace. Describes how the tests work, legal issues, setting up a program and how to avoid a false positive.

Drug Testing at Work explains what the tests can and can't determine and shows employers how to maintain a drug-free workplace without violating individual rights. Reveals techniques drug users use to beat the test and how employers can fight cheating.

Brain Boosters
Foods and Drugs That Make You Smarter

Beverly Potter, Ph.D.
Sebastian Orfali, M.A.
$12.95, 252 pp.
0-914171-65-8

Brain Boosters describes how the brain works and nutrients, herbs and pharmaceuticals that are reported to improve mental function. Reports the controversy the proposed FDA regulations and the "war over vitamins."

Brain Boosters chronicles the evolution of the "smart drinks." It explains the new nootropic smart drugs and how people order them from domestic and foreign sources.

Brain Boosters includes a directory of life-extension doctors. Professionals, business people, seniors, people concerned about Alzheimer's as well as parents, students, athletes and party-goers will find *Brain Boosters* a valuable resource on how to feed your brain for peak performance and a long, healthy life.

TO ORDER: Indicate the books you want, add up total, add 8.25% tax if shipped to California address, plus shipping fee. Send check or money order in U.S. dollars or Visa/MC number (with exp date and signature) and shipping info to: Ronin Publishing, Inc., P.O. Box 1035, Berkeley, Ca 94701, P 510-540-6278, F 510-548-7326, e—RoninPub@aol.com.

#	Title	Price	Ext
___	_____	___	___
___	_____	___	___
___	_____	___	___

SHIP TO:
NAME _____
COMPANY _____
ADDRESS _____
CITY _____ STATE _____ ZIP _____
PHONE _____

MC/VISA # _____/_____/_____/_____
EXP DATE _____/_____

    Subtotal _____
    Calif Tax _____
    Shipping* _____
    TOTAL _____

*SHIPPING:
    USA: $3 + $1 per item;
    Canada: $3 + $2 per item,

_____
    SIGNATURE

FROM

COOPERATION

HOW TO
MEDIATE A DISPUTE

Know someone caught in the middle?

Why not share *From Conflict to Cooperation* with your staff, team, association and friends? Order three or more copies and get a generous discount.

Discount & UPS Shipping Schedule*

Number	Discount	UPS
3 - 5	15%	$6
6 - 10	25%	$8
11 - 25	40%	$10
26 - 50	45%	$15
51 - 100	50%	actual
101+	call for discounts	

*terms & prices subject to change without notice

Wholesale Order Form

_____ copies of *From Conflict to Cooperation* @ $14.95 =   _____

Less discount   -_____

Subtotal   _____

Cal sales tax @ 8.25%*   _____

UPS shipping   _____

Total   _____

Ship to:

Name _____ Title _____

Company _____

Street _____

City_____ St._____ Zip _____

Phone _____ Fax _____ E _____

MC/VISA # _____/_____/_____/_____

EXP DATE _____/_____   * Resale # if exempt

_____   _____
SIGNATURE

Send completed Order Form and check or money order to Ronin Publishing, PO Box 1035, Berkeley, Ca 94701, or FAX to 510-548-7326. Allow 3-4 weeks delivery.

Dr. **Beverly Potter's** work blends humanistic psychology and Eastern philosophies with principles of behavior psychology to create an inspiring approach to the many challenges encountered in today's workplace. Beverly earned her Master's of Science in vocational rehabilitation counseling from San Francisco State and her Doctorate of Philosophy in counseling psychology from Stanford University. She was a member of the staff development team at Stanford for nearly twenty years. Beverly is a dynamic and informative speaker. Her workshops have been sponsored by numerous colleges including University of California at Berkeley Extension, San Francisco State Extended Education, DeAnza and Foothill Colleges Short Courses, as well as corporations such as Hewlett-Packard, Cisco Systems, Genentech, Sun Microsystems, Becton-Dickinson, and Tap Plastics; government agencies like California Disability Evaluation, Department of Energy, IRS Revenue Officers; and professional associations such as California Continuing Education of the Bar, Design Management Institute, and International Association of Personnel Women. Beverly has authored many books, including *Beating Job Burnout: How to Transform Work Pressure into Productivity, The Way of the Ronin: Riding the Waves of Change at Work, Turning Around: Keys to Motivation and Productivity, Preventing Job Burnout: A 50 Minute Workbook, Drug Testing at Work: A Guide for Employers and Employees,* and *Brain Boosters: Foods & Drugs that Make You Smarter.* Beverly is best known for her work on job burnout.